NATIVE TRIBES OF THE
SOUTHEAST

Michael Johnson
& Duncan Clarke

WORLD ALMANAC® LIBRARY

Please visit our web site at: **www.worldalmanaclibrary.com**
For a free color catalog describing World Almanac® Library's list
of high-quality books and multimedia programs, call 1-800-848-2928 (USA)
or 1-800-387-3178 (Canada). World Almanac® Library's fax: (414) 332-3567.

This North American edition first published in 2004 by
World Almanac® Library
330 West Olive Street, Suite 100
Milwaukee, WI 53212 USA

For Compendium Publishing
Contributors: Michael Johnson and Duncan Clarke
Editor: Michael Burke
Picture research: Michael Johnson and Simon Forty
Design: Tony Stocks/Compendium Design
Maps: Mark Franklin

World Almanac® Library editor: Barbara Kiely Miller
World Almanac® Library graphic designer: Steve Schraenkler

Picture credits
All artwork (other than maps) reproduced by kind permission of Richard Hook. All photographs are by Michael Johnson or supplied from his
collection unless credited otherwise below. Particular thanks are due to the staff of Royal Albert Memorial Museum and Art Gallery, Exeter,
Devon, U.K., for assistance and access to its exhibits, archives, and excellent collections, and to Bill Yenne for material of his own and from his
collection. Much of the material in this book appeared as part of *The Encyclopedia of Native Tribes of North America* by M. J. Johnson and
R. Hook, published by Compendium Publishing Ltd. in 2001.

Courtesy Alabama Department of Archives: p. 34; Cambridge University Museum of Archaeology and Anthropology, U.K.: front cover; Montclair
Art Museum, Montclair, New Jersey: p. 39; National Museum of the American Indian, Smithsonian Institution: pp. 23, 35; Royal Albert Memorial
Museum and Art Gallery: p. 30 (inset); Courtesy of the Royal College of Surgeons, London, U.K.: pp. 16, 17; Upton House, Warwickshire, U.K.: p.37;
Bill Yenne: pp. 4, 6, 8, 9, 12, 13, 26, 29, 30 (main picture), 40, 41, 57

Printed in the United States of America

1 2 3 4 5 6 7 8 9 08 07 06 05 04

Cover: Seminole group, Florida, c. 1895.

Previous page: Buckskin coat, probably Cherokee, c. 1830.

Contents

Introduction

Above: **The Native peoples who lived in the Ohio and Mississippi valleys are often referred to as Mound Builders because of their most visible legacy: large earth mounds that provided the first evidence of the existence of complex and sophisticated civilizations in North America.**

For thousands of years, the people known today as Native Americans or American Indians have inhabited the whole of the Americas, from Alaska to the southernmost tip of South America. Most scholars and anthropologists think that the ancestors of Native peoples came to the Americas from Asia over a land mass connecting Siberia and Alaska. These first Americans may have arrived as long as 30,000 years ago, although most historians estimate that this migration took place 15,000 years ago.

According to this theory, Paleo-Indians (*paleo*, from a Greek word meaning "ancient") migrated over many years down through an ice-free corridor in North America, spreading out from west to east and southward into Central and South America. In time, they inhabited the entire Western Hemisphere from north to south. Their descendants became the many diverse Native peoples encountered by European explorers and settlers.

"INDIANS" VS. "NATIVE AMERICANS"

Christopher Columbus is said to have "discovered" the Americas in 1492. But did he? Columbus was not the first European to visit what became known as the New World; Viking mariners had sailed to Greenland and Newfoundland almost five hundred years before and even founded short-lived colonies. Using the word "discovered" also ignores the fact that North America was already inhabited by Native civilizations whose ancestors had "discovered" the Americas for themselves.

When Columbus landed on an island he called San Salvador (Spanish for "Holy Savior"), he thought he had reached China or Japan. He had sailed west intending to get to the East—to Asia, or the fabled "Indies," as it was often called by Europeans of the time. Although he landed in the Bahamas, Columbus never really gave up on the idea that he had made it to the Indies. Thus when Native people first encountered Columbus and his men in the islands off Florida, the lost explorer called them "Indians." The original names that each tribal group had already given to themselves usually translate into English as "the people" or "human beings." Today, some Native people of North

America prefer to be called "American Indians," while others prefer "Native Americans." In this book, Native peoples will be referred to by their tribal names or, in more general cases, as "Indians."

Today's Indians are descended from cultures of great historical depth, diversity, and complexity. Their ancient ancestors, the Paleo-Indians, developed beliefs and behavior patterns that enabled them to survive in an unpredictable and often harsh environment. These early hunter-gatherers had a close relationship with the land, and a sense of absolute and eternal belonging to it. To them, everything in their world—trees, mountains, rivers, sky, animals, rock formations—had "spirit power," which they respected and placated through prayers and rituals in order to ensure their survival. These beliefs evolved over time into a fascinating and diverse series of creation stories, trickster tales, songs, prayers, and rituals passed down to and practiced by tribes throughout North America. Although many Indians today practice Christianity and other religions as well, many of their traditional songs, stories, dances, and other practices survive, on reservations and in areas where substantial tribal groups still live.

A CONTINENT OF CULTURES

Long before the Europeans arrived, important Indian cultures had already developed and disappeared. The ancient Adena and Hopewell people, for example, built a number of extraordinary burial mounds, and later even large towns, some of whose remains can still be seen at sites in the Midwest and South. These cultures were themselves gradually influenced by Mesoamerican (pre-Columbian Mexican and Central American) farming cultures based on growing maize (Indian corn), beans, and squash. They became the Mississippian culture from 700 A.D. The great spread of language groups across the North American continent also points to a rich Indian history of continual movement, invasion, migration, and conquest that took place long before European contact.

By the time the first European explorers and colonists set foot in North America, Indians had settled across the vast continent into different tribal groups and cultures that were active, energetic, and continually changing. American Indians were skilled in exploiting their particular

Above: **Much of the southeast from the Atlantic to the Mississippi was unbroken forest in the sixteenth century. Native tribes flourished and developed complex societies by tapping into the abundant supply of resources and game this environment provided.**

Above right: **The area covered in this book is the south Atlantic coast of the United States, the Gulf of Mexico, and west to the Mississippi and beyond. Note the "Indian Territory" area—see map on page 11.**

environments in a multitude of ways developed over time. They were also good at incorporating new methods and technologies from other peoples. When Europeans came, many Indians adapted the newcomers' technology to their own way of life, incorporating, for example, the horse, the rifle, money, beads, fabric, steel implements, and European-style agriculture into their own traditional cultures. In many cases, however, the benefits of European influence were eventually overshadowed by the displacement or outright destruction of traditional Native life.

WHAT THIS BOOK COVERS

The purpose of this book is to give some relevant facts about each of the main tribes native to the Southeast. Included here are brief historical sketches of the tribes, descriptions of tribal language relationships and groups, and accounts of traditional cultures, tribal locations, and populations in early and recent times. Interaction with invading Europeans is shown in discussions of trade, wars, treaties, and the eventual Indian removal to lands whose boundries served more to keep Indians in than to keep white settlwes out. Today's political boundaries were not recognized by Indians on their original lands; their "borders" were defined by the shifting of hunting, gathering, and farming that Native groups used and fought over. For ease of reference, however, tribal locations given here refer to modern U.S. and Canadian place names.

THE SOUTHEAST

The Indians of the southeastern United States—from Florida, Georgia, and the Carolinas west to Alabama, Mississippi, Louisiana, and neighboring states—were even more oriented toward agriculture than the Woodland tribes of the Northeast. They had the advantage of a more agreeable climate for farming and probably reflected the early Mesoamerican (Mexico and Central America) cultural influence. The first known ancestors of the southeastern tribes were the people of the Adena and Hopewell cultures, also called "Mound Builders." They left a strong legacy among the later Mississippians, whose descendants met the first European explorers. From the Mississippian culture, the southeastern tribes inherited agricultural practices, ritual and religious traits, and (among some tribes, such as

Southeast

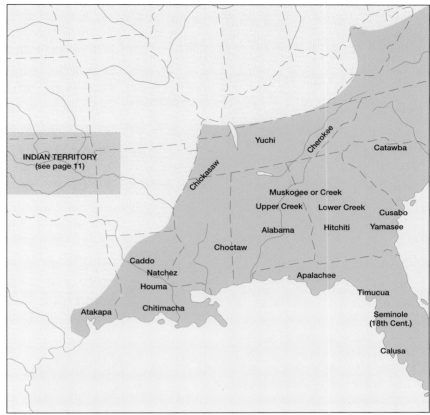

INDIAN TERRITORY
(see page 11)

Chickasaw

Yuchi

Cherokee

Catawba

Muskogee or Creek

Upper Creek   Lower Creek

Cusabo

Alabama   Hitchiti   Yamasee

Choctaw

Caddo

Natchez

Apalachee

Houma

Timucua

Atakapa   Chitimacha

Seminole
(18th Cent.)

Calusa

the Natchez) social class
systems of "honored men"
and common people. From
the Arawak and Carib of the
West Indies, the tribes living
along the Gulf of Mexico
inherited some Caribbean
traits, such as the use of
feather mantles, litters,
wooden stools, platform
beds, cane weaving, fish
poisoning, and blowguns.

The largest linguistic (or language) family of the
southeastern area was that of the Muskogean people,
including many small groups who were related to them. The
other main linguistic families were the Iroquoian, Caddoan,
and Siouan groups, plus a few tribes whose languages were
distinct and whose origins are largely unknown.

The land occupied by these tribes was almost unbroken
forest; once stretching from the Atlantic to the Mississippi
River, it provided a varied supply of nuts, berries, roots,
fish, and game to add to the agricultural produce of the
interior tribes. Their villages were clusters of reed- or bark-
covered dwellings, usually built along rivers and creeks,
with open central plazas or squares where the chiefs and
nobles lived close to the council and ritual houses.

These southern cultures were in pristine condition when
the French and Spanish explorers of the sixteenth and early
seventeenth centuries arrived. By the eighteenth century,
however, many of the coastal tribes had been ruined by
diseases and fighting with the Europeans, who had also
turned tribe against tribe in their colonial conflicts. For a

CENSUS 2000 FIGURES

Wherever possible U.S. Census
2000 figures are supplied with
each entry showing the number
of people who identified that
they were American Indian or
Alaskan Native and members of
only one tribe. Other people
reported as American Indian or
Alaskan Native in combination
with one or more other races
(defined in the census as
including white, black or
African-American, Native
Hawaiian, and other Pacific
Islander) and showing more
than one tribe of origin are
identified as "part. . . ."
Reporting variables mean that
some of the totals published
here may not be the precise
sum of the individual elements.

time the larger interior tribes maintained themselves fairly effectively by adopting European material culture. Their frontier life was reflected in their log cabin dwellings, Euro-American clothing, domesticated farm animals, and adoption of Christianity—the Cherokee even had their own newspaper and kept African slaves. This assimilation did not save them, however, from eventual removal to Indian Territory, now Oklahoma. A substantial number of Cherokee, Creek, Choctaw, Chickasaw, and Seminole still live there today, many with a mixed ancestry that includes whites and African-Americans. Some Cherokees were able to remain in North Carolina, as did some Choctaws in Mississippi, Seminoles in Florida, and a few Creeks in Alabama.

Below: **The main mounds of the Mississippi valley. While Cahokia was well past its prime when Europeans arrived on the continent (new construction ceased by 1450 and the site was abandoned by 1500), others were still important, particularly those of the Natchez tribe, which continued to build mounds into the seventeenth century.**

MOUND BUILDERS

The early peoples of the Southeast, centered in the Ohio and Mississippi valleys, are often referred to as Mound Builders because of their most visible legacy: large earth mounds that provided the first evidence of the existence of complex and sophisticated civilizations in North America. Archaeologists called the two main groups Adena and Hopewell, after the sites where their settlements were first investigated. Neither left written records, and they had long since disappeared when the first European settlers arrived. The Adena civilization flourished between about 800 B.C. and A.D. 200 in the Ohio Valley. The Hopewell, which also covered part of the Mississippi Valley, was prominent from around 300 B.C. to A.D. 700. Some argue that the Adena and Hopewell are actually a single complex culture, with some diverse patterns of art and culture developed over time.

Although much of the archaeological evidence was destroyed by early white settlers, who plowed over the mounds and other sites for farmland and dug up Indian artifacts to sell, enough remained to understand many aspects of the Mound Builders' lives. Both Adena and Hopewell peoples lived mainly in permanent villages. Elaborate copper ornaments and stamp-decorated pottery have been found throughout the region. The Adena built

burial mounds and large earthworks, some of which were in the shape of animals, apparently as part of their ritual practices for the dead. As with later peoples, it is thought that shamans—priests who were believed to communicate with the spirit world, often for purposes of healing—played an important role in their religious practices.

The Hopewell made earthen walls up to 10 feet (3 meters) high outlining squares, circles, and other geometric figures, as well as mounds of up to 30 feet (9 m) in height. Building work on this scale clearly indicates a sophisticated organization of labor resources and may be further evidence of ancient cultural links with Central American peoples who built pyramids, temples, and other complex structures. Early southeastern dwellers also engaged in long-distance trade, transferring coastal items such as shells and valued stone types throughout the region. Some mound building continued into the Mississippian period, lasting into the eighteenth century, with the Natchez people building temples and houses for god-kings on platform mounds.

Above and Above left: Cahokia—on the Mississippi opposite St. Louis—and Moundville in Alabama are the most famous of the Mississippian centers. Cahokia stretched over an area of more than 5 square miles (13 square kilometers) and the civilization that evolved here between the eleventh and thirteenth centuries A.D. probably sustained the largest prehistoric population north of Mexico. At Cahokia is the largest prehistoric earthwork in North America: Monk's Mound rises in four terraces to 100 feet (30 m).

INDIAN TERRITORY

This was the name given to a vast tract of land assigned by the U.S. government to settle Indians removed from their ancestral lands, mainly in the Southeast. In the 1820s, the so-called Five Civilized Tribes (the Cherokee, Creek, Seminole, Choctaw, and Chickasaw) of the Southeast were moved by the government to lands west of the Mississippi River. Under the Indian Removal Act of 1830, President Andrew Jackson received authority to designate specific lands for the expelled tribes, and the situation was formalized with the passage of the Indian Intercourse Act (1834). The Indian Territory included present-day Oklahoma to the north and east of the Red River, as well as parts of Kansas and Nebraska. In 1854, however, the creation of the Kansas and Nebraska Territories reduced the allotted land in favor of white settlers. Other tribes were also moved to Indian Territory, for a total of about forty groups in all.

Many people suffered terribly on the way west. They had been ruthlessly dispossessed and expelled to an unknown country far away. Many died from hunger and exhaustion during the journey, while others succumbed soon after their arrival, weakened by an ordeal that has become known as the "Trail of Tears." Once arrived in Indian Territory, each tribe was entitled to maintain its own separate government and customs as best as it could. In their native lands many groups, notably the Five Tribes, had by the 1830s adopted a way of life very much like that of white settlers, becoming small-scale farmers, often Christians, and even slave owners.

Rebuilding their lives after this tragedy, most Indian groups reestablished villages, small towns, and tribal institutions. Almost immediately, however, they came under pressure from land-hungry settlers. The Civil War divided tribes whose support was split between the Confederacy and the Union, while others futilely tried to remain neutral. Casualties among Indian soldiers were high, and looting and more land dispossession followed the Southern defeat. The opening of western Oklahoma to whites in 1889 was the first step in the extinction of the Indian Territory, which happened in 1907 when Oklahoma entered the Union. By the 1950s, much of the remaining Indian land had been lost, partly through fraud and excess taxation. Nevertheless, Oklahoma remains today the home of the majority of surviving Indian tribes of southeastern ancestry.

TRIBAL NAMES

Tribe	Meaning of name	Tribe	Meaning of name
Acolapissa	those who listen and see	Mobile	to paddle
Adai	–	Monacan	digging stick
Alabama	to camp, or weed gatherer	Moneton	big water people
Apalachee	people on the other side	Muskogee	swampy ground
Atakapa	man eaters	Nahyssan	–
Bayogoula	bayou people	Napochi	those who see
Biloxi	first people	Natchez	warriors of the high bluff
Calusa	fierce people	Natchitoches	paw paw tree
Cape Fear Indians	–	Ocaneechi	–
Catawba	separated or strong people	Ofo	dog people
Chakchiuma	red crawfish people	Pascagoula	bread people
Chatot	–	Pedee	something good
Cheraw	–	Pensacola	hair people
Cherokee	people of a different speech	Saponi	shallow water
Chickasaw	to leave	Seminole	separate, runaway, wild
Chitimacha	those who have pots	Sissipahaw	–
Choctaw	red or flat	Taensa (Natchez)	–
Cusabo	Coosawhatchie River people	Timucua	earth
Eno–Shakori	mean	Tunica	those who are the people
Hasinai	our own folk	Tuskegee	warrior
Hitchiti	to look upstream	Tutelo	–
Houma	red crawfish	Waccamaw	–
Kadohadacho	real chiefs	Wateree	–
Keyauwee	–	Yamasee	gentle
Koasati (Coushatta)	white cane	Yuchi	those far away, yonder
Manahoac	they are very merry		

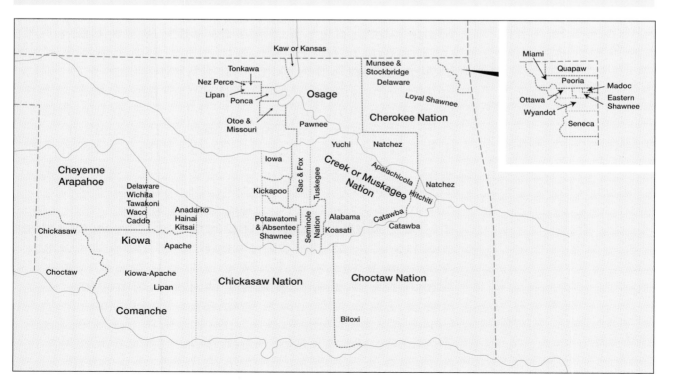

Above and Right: **The Alabama-Coushatta Powwow is a colorful and dramatic Pan-Indian event as these photos show.**

ALABAMA

A Muskogean tribe on the Alabama River close to its junction with the Coosa and Tallapoosa. The tribe probably absorbed two smaller ones who may have been closely related, the Tawasa, once on the Chattahoochee River, and the Pawokti of the Choctawhatchee River. After 1763, they began moving westward, leading ultimately to the establishment in 1854 of a reservation in Polk County, Texas, where they combined with the Coushatta. Some emigrated with the Creek to Indian Territory, where their descendants retain their identity near Weleetka, Okfuskee County. In 1700, they numbered perhaps 2,000; in 1944, 152 were reported as separate in Oklahoma, and 415 Alabama-Coushatta were reported from Polk County, Texas. The Alabama-Coushatta Tribes of Texas numbered 800 in 1990 and 882 in Census 2000.

COUSHATTA (KOASATI)

A Muskogean tribe closely related to the Alabama, whose later history is connected with the area at the junction of the Coosa and Tallapoosa Rivers, in Montgomery County, Alabama. The Muklasa, a neighboring group, may have been an associated tribe. During the eighteenth century, the Coushatta became politically part of the Upper Creek, and ultimately they were removed with the Creek to Oklahoma in the nineteenth century. Their descendants are found in Okfuskee and Hughes Counties. Before this move, however, a number of Coushatta had already settled on the Red, Sabine, Neches, and Trinity Rivers in Louisiana and Texas, a number later joined with the Polk County Alabama in Texas, and others settled in the Kinder-Elton area in Allen, Jefferson Davis, Washington, and St. Landry Parishes, Louisiana. The Oklahoma Coushatta numbered about 150 in 1950; the Louisiana Coushatta about 500 of mixed descent. Census 2000 reports 974, including 584 single-tribe respondents.

Above: **A Catawba group at Rock Hill, South Carolina, wearing modernized Indian clothes that their ancestors would never have known.**

T he Catawba (Katapu) were the largest of the Siouan tribes of the East, numbering about 6,000 in the early 1600s. The Catawba language seems to have formed a divergent Siouan branch with few close relations. Today they are the only representatives of the whole range of eastern Siouan tribes to survive to the twenty-first century under their old name. Some sources suggest that there was a merger of the Catawaba proper and a second group, named the Iswa, during the early years of their contact with Europeans. They probably first met the Spanish in 1566–67, and in 1701 encountered English explorer John Lawson along the Catawba River near the present state boundary between the Carolinas. By the 1750s, all the tribes in this region were in rapid decline due to the effect of imported alcohol and epidemics of smallpox and other non-Native diseases. The Catawba absorbed the surviving fragments of other tribes such as the Santee, Congaree, Waxhaw, Sewee, and Sugeree. Despite this, their numbers were drastically cut to around 500 or fewer individuals.

The Catawba constructed villages of circular, bark-covered pole-frame houses and larger temple structures, which they used for religious ceremonies and public gatherings. Both men and women played a role in agriculture. They harvested at least two crops of corn, beans, squash, and gourds each year, and supplemented their diet with hunting and fishing. The Catawba also ate acorns and other wild plant foods. They were skilled at making rush and grass baskets and pottery, which they decorated by using wood stamps before firing. Catawba chiefs wore headdresses of wild turkey feathers, while women in mourning dressed in clothes made from

tree moss. Blowguns, which fired 8-inch-
(20-centimeter-) long darts with an accurate range
of about 30 feet (9 m), were an important means
of hunting.

In almost constant conflict with the Iroquois and
Shawnee for decades, the Catawba were nevertheless
usually friendly with the English colonists of South
Carolina, aiding them against the Tuscarora in
1711–13, and later against the French and northern
Indians. Despite this alliance, British traders
regularly seized the wives and children of Catawba
warriors who could not pay trading debts and sold
them as slaves. Perhaps for this reason, the Catawba
joined in the general uprising of 1715 that became
known as the Yamasee War, but after it ended, the
survivors soon resumed relatively good relations
with the English settlers. By the time they served as
scouts during the Cherokee war, the Catawba could
field only around sixty warriors out of a population
of perhaps four or five hundred. Some served as
scouts for the colonists in the American Revolution.
They continued to decline in numbers, but in the
1850s, probably in recognition of past services,
they obtained a small reservation of 630 acres (255
hectares) in York County near Rock Hill, South
Carolina. A few Catawbas journeyed west during
the nineteenth century, and a few settled near
Scullyville, Oklahoma, a number in Arkansas,
and some with the Mormons in Colorado.

The York County Catawbas numbered 490 in 1780;
450 in 1822; 120 in 1881; 166 in 1930; and 300 in
1970. They are of mixed ancestry; the last full-blood,
Robert Lee Harris, died in 1954, and the last fluent
speaker of their language, Chief Sam Blue, in 1959.
By 1990, the Indian population on the reservation
had fallen to 124, but the tribe had received nonprofit
corporate status and was a federally recognized tribal
entity. The tribe filed legal claims for restitution of its
original 144,000-acre (58,000-ha) reservation granted
during the colonial era and in 1993 was awarded
compensation of $50 million. This may have had
an effect on the population of the Catawba Indian
Nation which numbered 1,725 in Census 2000.

CATAWBA POTTERY

Native Americans have been
making pottery for over 4,500
years. The Catawba have passed
the tradition from one generation
to the next and are the only
Indians east of the Great Pueblos
of New Mexico to continue the
ancient craft. They have kept the
purity of the ancient pottery and
do not use commercial clay,
potting wheels, glaze or paint.
Indeed, many people credit the
very survival of the Catawba to
their fine pottery.

The clay for the pottery comes
from secret sources along the
Catawba River. Their method of
working and mixing the clay is
another ancient and closely
guarded secret. Most of the
potters are women. The vessels
are built up by coils which are
then worked into shape.
Catawba pottery is never glazed
or painted but sometimes has
fine line drawings in traditional
pre-Columbian designs.

A large and important tribe who once occupied the southern Appalachian Mountains, the Great Smoky Mountains, and the valleys of the upper Kanawha, Savannah, Hiwassee, Tuckasegee, Coosa and Tennessee Rivers in present-day eastern Tennessee, western North Carolina, and northern Georgia and Alabama, comprising an area of 40,000 square miles (104,000 square kilometers). The capital of the nation seems to have been Echota, a settlement on the south bank of the Little Tennessee River. The Cherokee first encountered Europeans during Hernando De Soto's expedition in 1540, and they later held a great mountain area between the English settlements on the Atlantic coast and the French and Spanish garrisons along the Ohio and Mississippi. Unlike their distant relatives the Iroquois, with their confederated League of Five Nations, however, the Cherokee lacked the political cohesion to exert their power effectively and were often divided among themselves. Although the Cherokee may have separated from the Iroquois over two thousand years ago, they maintained a distant linguistic connection and seem to have spoken in a number of minor dialects.

The Cherokee had over sixty villages, which were connected to the outside world by seven main groups of trails. These allowed them to visit the Iroquois, Chickasaw, Catawba, and the Gulf tribes. Early Cherokee dwellings were built of poles covered inside and out with interwoven twigs or mixed clay and grass; and some housed several families. By the

Above and Left: **Cherokee men, purported to be Moses Price and Richard Justice, painted by William Hodges in London in 1790-91, when they accompanied William Augustus Bowles during an "unofficial" delegation of Creeks and Cherokee to England following the American Revolution, in an attempt to re-establish commercial and military activity between Great Britain and the southern tribes. Courtesy of the Royal College of Surgeons, London, U.K.**

Below: **Cherokee chief, c. 1825. The ceremonial dress of southeastern leaders at the time of their removal to Indian Territory mixed European materials with Native styles. This European-style coat has an open front and large collar; the cloth turban features a silver band and imported feathers. Some Cherokee, Creek, and Seminole triangular flap bandolier pouches survive, decorated in unique curving symmetrical beadwork designs of an almost African quality; one example has gold-plated beads.**

eighteenth century, however, the Cherokee had largely adopted the log cabin styles of white frontier settlers, along with other European material and social influences. At the center of each village was a circular council house where religious, political, and social gatherings took place. They farmed, growing corn (maize), beans, squash, pumpkins, and tobacco, activities largely controlled by the women. They also were gatherers, hunters, and skillful fishermen. They used bows and arrows and reed blowguns before the introduction of firearms. Pottery and basketry were expertly made, as were elaborately carved pipes, some of which have been preserved in museum collections. Pre-contact Cherokees imported shell wampum (ground and polished shell beads) that was used as currency, as well as kept for decorative beadwork. Their other important trade items were maple sugar and carved pipes. After Europeans introduced horses, pigs, and other farm animals, the Cherokee became accomplished at raising livestock.

The religious and political activities of the Cherokee people were governed by the White Peace Organization, and the rituals of war by the Red War Organization. Each had a complex round of ceremonies, including six great festivals held in the council house: Planting Corn, First Green Corn, and Ripe Green Corn, Feasts of the New Moon and of Reconciliation, the New Fire Rite, and Bounding Bush Feast. The Red War Organization arranged war parties and victory dances. They also held the ball game indigenous to eastern North America, a rough team game still played by Eastern Cherokees.

The Cherokee were mostly on the side of the French in the French and Indian War and on the side of the British in the Revolutionary War. They became the object of hatred for expansionary white settlers, and peace was not restored until 1794. From this time until their removal to Indian Territory, they suffered a period of increasing political pressure and cession of land, which resulted in groups of Cherokees moving to Arkansas and Texas. Finally, following the Treaty of New Echota in 1835, a large portion of the tribe, including most of those with mixed ancestry under Cherokee leader John Ross, were forcibly removed to Indian Territory during 1838–39. This journey involved intense suffering and the loss of a quarter of their people—an episode known ever since as "The Trail of Tears." A number of Cherokee escaped removal, and in 1889 a reservation was formally established around a number of conservative communities near the Great Smoky Mountains, North Carolina. This is known as the Qualla Reservation of the Eastern Cherokee.

The Western Cherokee of Indian Territory, now Oklahoma, contained the highest proportion of the most acculturated (practicing white ways) members of the tribe. They operated schools, newspapers, and churches and owned African-American slaves. They also included a number of conservatives (living traditionally) who had moved west ahead of the main body in 1838. The Western Cherokee had a quasi-national government and were known as one of the Five Civilized Tribes of Oklahoma.

The use of Sequoyah's alphabet in their schools during the nineteenth century was a major reason why the Cherokee rapidly became a literate people. Sequoyah was a mixed-blood Cherokee born in the 1770s in the village of Tuskegee on the Tennessee River. He began working on his writing system while recovering from a hunting accident and demonstrated it to tribal elders in 1812. Technically, it is what linguists call a syllabary rather than an alphabet, because the signs represent not single sounds but all the combinations of vowel and

Left: **Cherokee log cabin, c. 1840. Eighteenth-century association with Carolina settlers led to the gradual replacement of houses built of vertically set interwoven poles, covered inside and out with clay mixed with grass, by the log cabins typical of white frontiersmen. A few Eastern Cherokee in North Carolina still used stone-chimneyed log houses until recent times.**

consonant sounds that form the Cherokee language. Within a year, reading and writing in the Cherokee language had spread widely. In 1828, the *Cherokee Phoenix*, or *Tsa la gi Tsu lehisanunhi*, funded by the tribal council, became the first Indian newspaper published in the United States.

As supporters of the Confederacy during the Civil War, the Western Cherokee suffered war casualties and retribution under the Reconstruction Treaty of 1866, but they have maintained a substantial population within their old area in northeastern Oklahoma. In 1920, 36,432 Cherokees were reported in Oklahoma and in 1930, 45,238; in recent years they were reported as numbering 66,150, which included the Eastern band, separately reported as 1,963 in 1930. The Oklahoma Cherokee today are largely of mixed descent and live

predominantly in Cherokee, Adair, and Delaware Counties, particularly around Tahlequah, their nineteenth-century capital. Members of the tribe live throughout the state and across the country, however, and have become, for the most part, one of the best integrated Indian people in American society.

The Eastern Cherokee were a more conservative portion of the tribe until recent times. The present population is about 8,000, with a number of relatively full-blood communities. They have retained the Ball Game (each player uses two racket-type sticks to catch a small ball made of deer hide and hair, the object being to hit the goal or the wooden fish at the top with the ball). Old games,

Above: **A Cherokee woman, of the Eastern band, North Carolina, molds pots out of clay by hand, c. 1950.**

Opposite: **A buckskin coat, probably Cherokee, c. 1830. This buckskin coat follows American frontier style and is formed with silk or thread embroidery. Formerly W. Reid Collection**

dances, and basketry are seen at their annual Cherokee Indian Fair; and they operate a reconstructed "Oconaluftee Indian Village" and Museum. In recent years, however, a more dominant group with diverse ancestry in the main Cherokee village has exploited the local tourist trade by providing inauthentic Indian attractions. Both Eastern and Western Cherokees also operate outdoor dramas, called Unto These Hills, to show their own version of Cherokee history. Besides the two main bodies of the tribe, substantial numbers of rural people—in Tennessee particularly—also claim Cherokee ancestry. In 1990, the Cherokees were reported to number 122,000, and many more claimed their ancestry; 13,000 still spoke their language, a dialect known as Atali or Overhill in Oklahoma, one of the few thriving

Above: **Tachee, a Texas Cherokee chief also called "Dutch," who moved west with his band ahead of the main Cherokee removal. From a lithograph published by McKenney & Hall, 1836–44.**

Indian tongues outside the Southwest. Another Cherokee dialect, called Middle or Kituhwa, is spoken by around 1,000 people in North Carolina, although its use is mainly confined to church services. All three groups, the Eastern Band of Cherokee Indians, the Cherokee Nation of Oklahoma, and the United Keetowah Band, are all federally recognized as tribal entities, while another fifty or so groups across twelve states claim Cherokee descent and identity. The United Keetowah Band was formed in the 1930s by a group opposed to assimilation. It revived many traditional cultural practices, receiving federal recognition in 1946. For Census 2000 figures see the box on page 19.

Economic activities on Cherokee land today include oil and gas sales, gaming, ranching and logging, and arts and crafts. Additionally, there are both Native-owned and non-Native tourist facilities offering employment opportunities.

Above: **A Cherokee beaded bandolier, reported to have been given by Sam Houston to General Jackson, c. 1830. National Museum of the American Indian, Smithsonian Institution**

A CHEROKEE CREATION LEGEND

Long ago when all was water, the animals lived above but it was very crowded and they wanted more room. Dayunisi, the little Water-beetle, volunteered to go see what was below the water. It dived again and again to the bottom and each time came up with soft mud that he used to form the island we call Earth, suspended by cords at each of the cardinal points to the solid rock of the sky. The Great Buzzard, the father of all birds, flew down close to the earth while it was still soft. He became tired and his wings began to strike the ground. Where they struck the earth became a valley and where they rose up again became a mountain and in this way the landscape of the Cherokee country was created. Men came to the new land after the animals and plants. First there were only two humans, a brother and a sister. Then he struck her with a fish and told her to multiply. After seven days she gave birth to a child, then another and another every seven days. Then it was made that a woman should have only one child in a year, and this has been the way since that time.

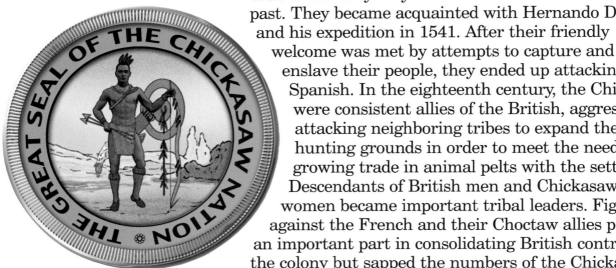

An important tribe of the Muskogean language family, the Chickasaw lived in northern Mississippi, Tennessee, and Arkansas, and at one time along the Tennessee River in northern Alabama. They were culturally similar to the Choctaw, with whom they may have been united in the distant past. They became acquainted with Hernando De Soto and his expedition in 1541. After their friendly welcome was met by attempts to capture and enslave their people, they ended up attacking the Spanish. In the eighteenth century, the Chickasaw were consistent allies of the British, aggressively attacking neighboring tribes to expand their hunting grounds in order to meet the needs of a growing trade in animal pelts with the settlers. Descendants of British men and Chickasaw women became important tribal leaders. Fighting against the French and their Choctaw allies played an important part in consolidating British control over the colony but sapped the numbers of the Chickasaw, as did outbreaks of disease. The Chickasaw were enthusiastic fighters and raiders who fiercely repelled invasions of their territory by other Indians, at least up to the time of the American Revolution. Small bands of warriors carried with them a sacred war medicine bundle, adding its powers to their own ritual preparations to enhance their fighting skill.

Each clan had a chief, with a senior chief chosen from the Minko clan known as the High Minko. Religion focused on a supreme deity called Ababinili, who was a composite of four celestial entities: Sun, Clouds, Clear Sky, and He That Lives in the Clear Sky. There were two high priests, called *hopaye*, who led religious ceremonies. Healers used natural medicines to combat illness caused by evil spirits.

The Chickasaw built their villages on hills and often surrounded them with wooden palisade fences for defense against enemy raiders. Their pole-framed houses had clapboard sides and were painted both inside and out using a whitewash made from clay or powdered shells. In winter they sought shelter from the

Above: **The Great Seal of the Chickasaw Nation—see box opposite. There are well over 500 officially recognized Native American tribes today, and many have official seals with fascinating stories attached to them.**

colder weather by living in semi-subterranean circular houses with bark or thatch roofs. Inside were raised wood-frame beds. The staple foods of the Chickasaw were the regular crops of the southeastern Indians—corn, beans, squash, and sunflower seeds. Women also gathered foods such as nuts, acorns, honey, and wild onions. This diet was supplemented by hunting and fishing; they stunned fish using green walnut poison. The Chickasaw developed their own breed of horse from early animals stolen from the Spanish or traded from other groups. Women wove cloth from the inner bark of the mulberry, decorating it with human and animal figures as well as geometric designs.

In the early nineteenth century, the Chickasaw largely abandoned their old lifestyle to become farmers, in some cases with small cotton plantations. Members of the tribe acquired a total of around 1,000 African-American slaves. Under pressure from ever-increasing numbers of whites, they gradually ceded (gave up) their lands to Euro-American settlers and were pushed farther west. All tribal lands east of the Mississippi were ceded in 1832, and between 1836 and 1847, about 3,000 Chickasaws were removed to Indian Territory (Oklahoma). Many died of disease, hunger, and attacks by Plains Indians, but the survivors formed one of the so-called Five Civilized Tribes and were able to rebuild their lives as farmers.

The Chickasaw formed a self-governing nation with a capital in Tishomingo until the Civil War. During this period they seem to have completed the transition to Euro-American rural culture, with many of the remnants of Native culture, dress, and ancient institutions falling into disuse. The reservation that was established in 1855 was abolished when Oklahoma became a state in 1907. The tribal government was also abolished, and the land was allocated to individual Indians. By 1920, the tribe retained only some 300 acres (121 ha) out of the 4.7 million (1.9 million ha) they originally had. Their descendants live in several Oklahoma counties, particularly Pontotoc, Johnston, and Love, and in adjacent towns and cities. They are today largely of mixed ancestry, numbering 4,204 in 1910, 5,616 in 1970, and 20,887 in Census 2000. Most are Methodists or Baptists; about 500 still speak the Chickasaw language.

THE GREAT SEAL

The Chickasaw nation was formally created on March 4, 1856, in Tishomingo, Oklahoma, and the Great Seal was attached to all legal papers produced from 1867 until 1907, when the state of Oklahoma was formed. In recent times the seal is again being attached to all important Chickasaw documents.

The gold outer rim of the seal stands for the purity of the Chickasaw people, and the pale purple inner ring for their honor. The warrior on the seal is Tishomingo, the last of the great war chiefs before the nation moved west. Tishomingo represents the courage of the Chickasaw. Behind him flows the Mississippi River (which means "without source" in ancient Chickasaw) and he is surrounded by local plants and trees to remind the Chickasaw of their ancestral lands. The arrows he holds represent the two divisions of ancient Chickasaw society, those who lived in the woods and the larger group that lived in the fortified towns. His headfeathers signify the four directions of the earth. He is wearing the traditional decoration of great warriors, the Warrior's Mantle of swan feathers. His deer-hide shield shows how he protects his people while his hickory bow attests to his great hunting ability and how well he provides food. The quiver similarly represents the Chickasaws' hunting skills and their willingness to fight to defend their people.

Above: **Chitimacha dancers at a powwow—their tribal traditions are maintained, although the Chitimacha language is no longer spoken.**

Above right: **A split-cane basket, made by Lydla Darden, Chitimacha, Louisiana, 1972. The Chitimacha were known for producing the best baskets in the Gulf region.**

A group of three tribes forming a linguistic family who lived in Louisiana on the shores of Grand Lake, plus parts of the coast and delta regions of the Mississippi River: the Chitimacha proper on Grand Lake, the Chawasha on Bayou La Fourche, and the Washa in Assumption Parish. The name Chitimacha has been translated as "those living on the Grand River," as "those who have pots," or as "men altogether red." Linguists have linked them with the Tunica and Atakapa tribes and their languages into a "Tunican stock" (perhaps distantly related to the Muskogean languages), but the relationships are still not fully understood. The Chitimacha seem to have lived in their present locations for thousands of years, with archaeological evidence indicating that Bayou Teche in Louisiana has been continuously occupied since at least 800 B.C. by Native peoples with cultural characteristics similar to those of the Chitimacha.

In pre-French times, the Chitimacha lived in about fifteen villages, each with around 500 inhabitants, under the authority of a chief who gave allegiance to the Grand Chief residing in a village near Charenton, Louisiana. They had a noble class, consisting mainly of priests, headmen, and healers. Similar to others along the lower Mississippi, their houses were made of palmetto leaves over a framework of poles. They hunted deer with bow and arrow or blowguns with cane darts, collected vegetable foods, and planted corn (maize) and sweet potatoes. Shellfish were a particularly important part of the Chitimacha diet, and huge mounds of discarded shells have been found on the site of old villages. On Grand Lake there was a 12-square-foot (1-square-meter) temple that was the center for Chitimacha religious rituals, the most important of which was a six-day-long midsummer festival during which men were initiated through fasting and dancing. The dead were exposed on scaffolds, where it was the responsibility of people called Turkey Buzzard Men to clean off the flesh and return the bones to the family for burial under a mound. The Chitimacha are famous for their black and yellow cane basketry work. They used a special double weave technique that allows different patterns to be seen on the outside and the inside. Despite the painstaking and slow process involved, a few women continued the craft until recent times.

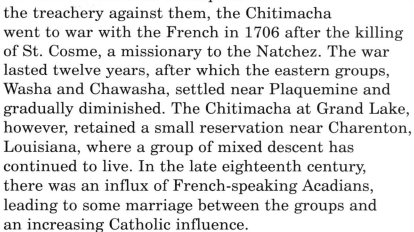

Although their isolated location offered the Chitimacha some protection from the worst effects of the Spanish incursion into the Southeast, by 1680 it is likely that imported diseases had already reduced their population to around half the pre-contact total. The Chitimacha were raided for slaves by French settlers from the earliest contacts. In response to the treachery against them, the Chitimacha went to war with the French in 1706 after the killing of St. Cosme, a missionary to the Natchez. The war lasted twelve years, after which the eastern groups, Washa and Chawasha, settled near Plaquemine and gradually diminished. The Chitimacha at Grand Lake, however, retained a small reservation near Charenton, Louisiana, where a group of mixed descent has continued to live. In the late eighteenth century, there was an influx of French-speaking Acadians, leading to some marriage between the groups and an increasing Catholic influence.

The entire population of the Chitimacha may have exceeded 3,000 in 1650. Only a few hundred remained by the start of the nineteenth century, and even that number was drastically reduced in 1855 by a yellow fever epidemic. The census of 1910 recorded only 69 Chitimachas, and that of 1930, 51. The Bureau of Indian Affairs (BIA) reported 89 living on the Chitimacha Reservation, St. Marys Parish, in 1950, although a recent total count in the early 1990s, including all descendants, found 720 enrolled members. Census 2000 reported 1,001 members. Today the tribe is federally recognized and there is a BIA school on the reservation. Most Chitimachas work in the oil or fishing industries, and part of the small reservation is leased to oil companies. There is a museum and cultural complex, but the Chitimacha language is no longer spoken.

TOURIST AND SOUVENIR TRADE

Native artists throughout North America often used their talents to produce beautifully decorated objects in their traditional manner for the white souvenir market. Eastern tribes were producing quill-decorated bark objects from the eighteenth century onwards. Beadwork became very popular with white curio seekers during the nineteenth century. Baskets were collected from Southwestern, West Coast and California tribes. Such crafts helped many Indian people living in poverty, although their wares often sold at a fraction of their true value.

The largest tribe of the Muskogean language family, the Choctaw lived in the south and center of the present state of Mississippi. They are thought to be descendants of the Mound Builders and are closely related culturally to the Chickasaw. Like the Creek, they grew corn as a staple crop in farms along the lower Mississippi as well as beans, pumpkins, melons, and sunflowers. Men fished and hunted for buffalo, deer, bear, and small game. In the seventeenth century, there were over a hundred Choctaw villages, some of them fortified, especially in border areas near hostile tribes. Houses were pole-frame structures with roofs made of grass or reed thatch and walls of bark, hide, or matting. In winter, they lived in circular houses that were insulated with clay walls. Towns had a chief and a war chief, although these were junior to district chiefs. There was no central tribal authority except a tribal council that met extremely infrequently. One way they settled disputes, as well as an important source of entertainment, was the sport of lacrosse, which was played using balls made from deerskin and animal thong nets. Ritual preparations were vital to a successful event, which could involve either male or female teams. Choctaw dress was similar to that of

Below: **A split-cane basket made by a Choctaw tribe member, Elton, Louisiana, 1974.**

other southeastern tribes: skirts, tunics, and loincloths of deerskin and robes made from bear or buffalo hides. Buffalo wool was spun and woven together with plant fibers to make cloth used for skirts. Their most important arts were verbal, with singing and poetry being highly valued. They also made fine baskets, and some men were skilled wood carvers, making elaborate decorations for mortuary buildings.

The Choctaw's first contact with Europeans came with the passage through their territory of Spanish explorers led by Hernando De Soto, who destroyed several Choctaw villages in 1540. Over a century passed before they were again contacted by whites, as the arrival of French explorer Pierre Le Moyne d'Iberville heralded French settlement in the region that would become Louisiana. By the late 1600s, the Choctaw had become close allies with the French colony in their struggles with the Chickasaw and the British. They fought alongside the French in the defeat of the Natchez revolt in 1729, and conflict with the Creek and Chickasaw continued long after the French had ceded their lands to British control.

During the American Revolution, Choctaw warriors served on the side of the colonists; and in the War of 1812, they fought with Andrew Jackson against the Creeks. Throughout this period many

Above: **A 1910 postcard showing a Choctaw girl.**

Choctaws died from the effects of alcohol and imported diseases, while much land was lost to white settlers. In 1805, they began a series of treaties with the United States. Finally, in 1830, at the Treaty of Dancing Rabbit Creek, they finally ceded most of their remaining lands in Mississippi and were forced to leave for new lands in Indian Territory, now Oklahoma. At least 12,000 Choctaw were sent on the journey of several hundred miles, and around a quarter died along the way from the effects of disease, hunger, or exhaustion. Others who escaped the initial roundup were removed later. By 1838, the surviving Choctaws (one of the so-called Five Civilized Tribes) had established a separate form of government in Indian Territory based at Tuskahoma, until it too was absorbed into the state of Oklahoma after 1907.

Before removal west, the Choctaw had partly adopted a Euro-American culture, growing garden vegetables, raising poultry, hogs, cattle, and horses, and wearing European clothing. The process begun in Mississippi continued during the nineteenth century, so that little Native culture remained. Not all Choctaws moved to Oklahoma, however. Despite continued persecution, a substantial number managed to maintain themselves in several communities in Mississippi, at Pearl River, Tucker, and Bogue Chitto, Neshoba County; Red Water and Standing Pine, Leake County; Conehatta, Newton County; and Bogue Homo in Jones County. Today a few also live near Jena and other places in Louisiana.

The Civil War was a further tragedy for the Choctaw and the other tribes of Indian Territory, as their support for the Confederacy led to both heavy loss of life and harsh retaliation. Former African-American slaves were eventually adopted into the tribe. Indian Territory tribes lost most of their lands in the late nineteenth century, with the transformation of the Territory into the state of Oklahoma in 1907, ending their remaining legal independence.

Left and Below: **Choctaw ball game player. George Catlin recorded the face paint, broad decorated belt, and horsetail ornaments in c. 1830. Known in both the northeastern and southeastern woodlands, this team game was often played violently as a substitute for war. In recent times the Iroquois used one racquet (see Inset, left), the Choctaw and Cherokee two.**

Above: **Louisiana Choctaw woman with large burden basket on a chest tumpline, c. 1880. Almost all eastern basketry used the simple plaiting technique and available materials. The Choctaw and Creek made fine river cane baskets of this "cow nose" shape; the Chitimacha made colorful baskets of narrow cane splints; the Cherokee and Catawba mainly used oak splints, and the northeastern tribes, ash.**

Today there are three federally recognized Choctaw tribal entities: the Choctaw Nation of Oklahoma, the Jena Band of Choctaw in Louisiana, and the Mississippi Band of Choctaw. Other groups in Louisiana and Alabama (such as the Mowa Band who have a small reservation in Mt. Vernon) are still seeking recognition. The present Oklahoma Choctaws live principally in McCurtain, Pittsburg, Le Flore, Pushmataha, and Choctaw Counties, and in many towns and cities of southeastern Oklahoma. They were reported to number 19,000 in 1944. The Oklahoma Choctaws are largely of mixed descent, with some white and African-American ancestry. The Mississippi Choctaws were reported as numbering about 3,000 in 1950. A combined census of 23,562 in 1970 included Oklahoma, Mississippi, and Louisiana Choctaws. That figure had risen by the time of Census 2000 to 87,349 (see box below).

Most Choctaws, both in Oklahoma and in Mississippi, are Baptists, with some hymns sung in the Choctaw language, although it is unlikely that there are still fluent speakers in Oklahoma (a few elderly people still use the language on the Mississippi reservations). Annual festivals, held on Labor Day in Oklahoma, are an important occasion for traditional dances, foods, and games, including lacrosse. Economic resources include gaming facilities, some factories, and in Mississippi, timber concessions. There is a tribal museum, a monthly paper, *Bishinik*, and an official web site.

CENSUS 2000

The numbers recorded for the Choctaw were:

Choctaw	66,287
Clifton Choctaw	76
Jena Band of Choctaw	84
Mississippi Band of Choctaw	7,626
Mowa Band of Choctaw	1,572
Oklahoma Choctaw	11,690
Total	87,349

The Lumbee today have some 40,000 to 50,000 members, making them the largest Indian nation east of the Mississippi and around the ninth largest in the United States, but the obscure nature of their ancestry has meant they are struggling to obtain full recognition from the BIA.

The earliest record of the Lumbee is from the first part of the eighteenth century, when they were recorded as speaking English and living as poor farmers in much the same fashion as the surrounding white settlers. Later that century they were displaced from much of their land by Highland Scots settlers. In 1790, the U. S. Census listed prominent Lumbee family names, including Locklear, Oxendine, Chavis, Lowry, Hammonds, and Kerseys, under "All other free persons." All were *disenfranchised* (deprived of the right to vote) and banned from carrying arms by the state of North Carolina in 1835.

During the Civil War, the Lumbee tried to resist efforts to conscript them into forced labor gangs. Led by Henry Berry Lowry (or Lowrie), they raided nearby plantations for food. Lowry escaped capture even after the war, when he was regarded by the Reconstruction authorities as a bandit, and finally disappeared from sight in 1872. From 1885 onward, the Lumbee have been officially recognized by the North Carolina state authorities, although under various names reflecting their uncertain origins. In 1885, they were listed as Croatoan Indians, in 1911 as Robeson County Indians, briefly as Cherokee Indians of Robeson County (withdrawn after Cherokee protests), and finally from 1953 as Lumbee Indians. The federal government acknowledged the Lumbee in 1956 but so far has denied them full recognition, and so they do not receive the benefits and subsidies given to officially recognized tribes. In 1958, the Lumbees drove the Ku Klux Klan out of Robeson County. They continued to be small-scale farmers long into the twentieth century and today hold a wide range of occupations in the area. Census 2000 reports 57,868, including 5,955 part Lumbee.

LUMBEE ORIGINS

The name Lumbee comes from the Lumber River. Since the colonial era, the Lumbee have lived in the marshy lands around the Lumber and Pee Dee Rivers in Robeson County in southeastern North Carolina. This remote area seems to have served as a refuge for displaced Indians of the Cheraw and perhaps also some Cherokee, Tuscarora, and Croatoan Indians. It also may be that some Lumbee are descendants of British settlers from the "lost" colony of Roanoke, Virginia (1587), absorbed by the Croatoan. Today there are at least twenty surnames of Roanoke colonists preserved among the Lumbee.

There are also communities of Lumbee living in Baltimore, Philadelphia, and Detroit. Most belong to Indian Protestant churches. A Lumbee River Regional Development Association was formed in 1968. Today the tribe organizes annual cultural events and continues to campaign for full federal recognition.

MUSKOGEE (CREEK)

Below: **William McIntosh, son of a Scottish trader and a Creek woman, became a leader of the pro-American faction of the Creek people at the time of the British-American conflict of 1812. Some of his followers aided the Americans against the Creeks at Atasi in 1813 and at Horseshoe Bend in 1814. His agreement to the sale of Creek lands to the Americans in 1823 led to his murder in 1825 for "selling the graves of their ancestors." The painting was done in 1820, although some doubt exists about the artist's name.**

One of the largest and most important groups of the Muskogean family, comprising a loose confederacy of tribes closely related by language in Georgia and Alabama, called "Creeks" by the British, an allusion to their villages being located close to rivers and creeks. They were generally divided into two branches. The "Upper Creeks" of Alabama were centered along the Alabama, Coosa, and Tallapoosa Rivers. This group comprised the Coosa and Tulsa in Tallapoosa County; the Abihka in Talladega County; the Atasi, Macon County; the Pakana and Tukabahchee, Elmore County; the Hilibi, Tallapoosa County; the Holiwahali (who probably included the Kolomi, Fus-Hatchee, and Kanhatki) in Elmore and Montgomery Counties; and the Okchai and Wakokai in Coosa County. The "Lower Creeks" resided chiefly east of the Chattahoochee River in Georgia and comprised the Kasihta close to the present site of Columbus, Georgia; the Coweta on the Ocmulgee River, who later moved near Columbus; and the Eufaula in Clay County, Georgia, and Talladega County, Alabama (some also emigrated to Florida and joined the Seminoles). Both Creek and non-Creek tribes formed a loose alliance that dated back at least to the 1500s and is known as the Creek Confederacy. During the eighteenth century, both the Upper and Lower groups were reinforced by other local Muskogean groups. The Alabama and Coushatta affiliated with the Upper Creek, while the Hitchiti groups joined the Lower Creek, and the non-Muskogean Yuchi and Shawnee also joined the confederacy at various times.

The Creek and Muskogeans generally were heirs of Mississippian horticulture, involving the planting of corn (maize), beans, cane, millet, tobacco, and sunflowers. They gathered nuts and wild fruits, hunted deer and bison (buffalo) in the west, and stored nut oil and bear fat. Their settlements were composed of a main town with small, sometimes palisaded, villages surrounding it. The towns contained a "square" where public and religious gatherings were held. Most tribes were divided into what anthropologists would call matrilineal totemic clans. This means that people were divided into groups associated with specific animals or birds, and that they took their membership from the clan of their mother. They constructed houses of logs and poles with mud or thatched roofs. From the early eighteenth century onward, they adopted log cabins of the white frontier type, along with a considerable amount of Euro-American material culture.

The Green Corn festival, or Busk, was a major religious rite, a form of which still survives among a number of conservative Oklahoma Creek communities. The Busk, a ceremony of thanksgiving and renewal, began with ritual purging through the drinking of a caffeine potion that caused vomiting. Then

This page: **Creek or Seminole beaded bandolier bag, c. 1820. A prestige bag with a shoulder strap, bandolier bags were worn by men and sometimes women at tribal dances.**

Right: **William Augustus Bowles, an American Loyalist at the time of the American Revolution, married into the Lower Creek and visited Great Britain twice in the 1790s. Painted by Thomas Hardy while in London, wearing wampum and other dress accessories of the Creek Indians of the period.**

there was dancing, feasting, music, and games, followed by a communal bath and a speech from the chief. Each town or small tribe elected a chief or micco, who was able to exercise influence over the consensus decisions of the town council, which decided all significant matters. The council, which included a group of elders known as the Beloved Men, met daily in the square or the town house. Certain towns were consecrated to peace and were designated "white towns." Others, set apart for war ceremonies, were designated as "red towns." From a method of time-keeping with sticks to record the days a war party might be on the trail, the term "Red Stick Creeks" was sometimes used by whites.

Their history of contact with whites begins with Hernando De Soto's expedition in 1540, and further Spanish contacts were made in 1559 and 1567. Later the Creeks became at first enemies but eventually allies of the British colonies of South Carolina and Georgia, and aided the British against the Apalachee (1703–08), the Choctaw, the Cherokee, and the colony of Spanish Florida. Creeks were keen fighters, with men classed as "war chiefs," "big warriors," or "little warriors" depending on their achievements in past war parties. Warriors painted their bodies with black and red pigments.

Fighting alongside the British gave the Creeks little protection from enslavement and other attacks from the settlers, as well as from the devastating impact of disease, so many joined the uprising known as the Yamasee War in 1715. A prominent Creek of mixed ancestry named Alexander McGillivray signed a treaty accepting U.S. protection in 1790, but the agreement was repudiated by other confederacy leaders. After the Revolution, constant hostilities with Americans climaxed in the Creek War of 1813–14, with the defeat and submission of William Weatherford, their principal leader, followed by the cession of a greater part of their lands to the United States. In 1832, they finally agreed to move to new lands in the West— Indian Territory, now Oklahoma—and in 1836, the majority of Creeks made the journey, by land and

river, in appalling conditions and at great cost in lives.

With remarkable fortitude, they adjusted to their new rich soil lands along the Arkansas River and organized a quasi-government at Okmulgee with a legislature composed of two houses—the House of Kings and the House of Warriors. Those whose ancestry included early European traders claimed the largest tracts of good farming lands, while the poorer, full-blooded Creeks sought the rural back country. The Civil War disrupted the Creek, one of the so-called Five Civilized Tribes. As slaveholders they were mostly drawn in on the Southern side and subsequently lost many possessions as whites pillaged their country. After the Dawes Act in the 1880s allowed tribal lands to be "allotted," with some land opened to white settlement, a substantial proportion of Creek lands passed to whites. Some Creeks continued to compromise with the federal government, despite the loss of their remaining lands and tribal leadership when Oklahoma attained statehood in 1907. Others resisted as best they could, with a rebellion against land allotment in 1900 led by an Upper Creek called Crazy Snake, and Creek participation alongside African-Americans and poor whites in what is known as the Green Corn Rebellion of 1917.

The present descendants of the Creeks and their associates are in McIntosh, Hughes, Okmulgee, Creek, and Muskogee Counties, Oklahoma, formerly the Creek Nation; also in the cities of Tulsa and Sapulpa, and throughout Oklahoma and the United States. Their population

Above: **A Creek man wearing the mixed Euro-American and Indian clothing of the early nineteenth century, before the Creek removal to Indian Territory. Painting by Lukas Visches, 1824**

prior to their removal from Georgia and Alabama was about 22,500; in 1857 they were reported to number 14,888. Later figures have been confused by the division into full-bloods, Creeks by "blood," African-American freedmen, and intermarried whites. In 1930, 8,760 were reported from Oklahoma; in 1950, 9,752; and in 1970, 17,004, including Alabama and Coushatta. A few descendants of those who remained in the East live near Atmore, in southern Alabama. In 1990, the Creeks were reported to number over 28,000, of which 16,000 were in Oklahoma and 1,800 were Poarch-Creeks near Atmore, Alabama. There are five federally recognized tribal entities, the largest being the Creek Nation of Oklahoma, and numerous small, as yet unrecognized Creek groups, some in Georgia and Florida.

The Creek Nation holds almost 150,000 acres in trust, with farming, gaming facilities, and the tribal government providing the main sources of employment. Cultural activities include a museum and an annual festival and rodeo, while aspects of Creek tradition continue to be preserved in some of the more remote rural communities.

Above: **Three cloth bandolier bags of Seminole, Creek, or Cherokee origin, c. 1830. All are decorated with beadwork, although the interpretations of the designs are unknown. Symbolic figures in abstract form are known to have been incorporated in similar bead embroidery from this period.**

THE MUSKOGEAN LANGUAGE FAMILY

This language family constituted one of the largest on the North American continent and was dominant in the southeastern area. Muskogean languages seem to fall into several dialectic divisions and among a large number of tribes. The extent and relationships among these dialects are still the subjects of considerable debate, since the movements of Muskogean-speaking people were so numerous between initial contact with the Spanish in the sixteenth century and their more extensive contacts with the French and British in the eighteenth century.

The dialectic groups were perhaps: (A) the Apalachee and their associates in northern Florida; (B) Hitchiti, mostly in central Georgia, later becoming Lower Creeks; (C) Alabama in Alabama State, later becoming Upper Creeks; (D) Choctaw and Chickasaw in Mississippi; (E) Tuskegee, Upper Creeks; (F) Yamasee-Cusabo; (G) Muskogee of Alabama and Georgia; then more diversely, (H) the Natchez of Mississippi, and (I) Calusa of Florida. The Muskogean linguistic family has in turn been distantly linked to the Tumucua, Yuchi, and Tunican families, and more improbably to the Iroquois and Caddoans. The true Muskogeans had crystallized into the Creek, Seminole, Choctaw, and Chickasaw by the early nineteenth century, when they were removed to Indian Territory, now Oklahoma.

The Natchez were the largest of a group of three tribes, including the Taensa and Avoyel, who spoke a divergent language of the Muskogean family, living close to the present site of the city of Natchez, Mississippi. Numbering perhaps 4,000, they were the most powerful tribe on the Mississippi in the 1650s. By the middle of the following century, however, only a few hundred survived, and the tribe effectively died out in the twentieth century.

The Natchez were descendants of the Mississippian Mound Builder culture, with a complex system of castes or ranked social groups made up of suns, nobles, honored men, and commoners or "stinkards." The sun was the supreme god, and he was represented on earth by a hereditary king, called the Great Sun. He wore a crown made from red tasseled swan feathers and was seated on a throne on a high mound each day to direct sun ceremonies. Other adobe mounds were the sites of a sun temple and the house of the king. In the temple, eight officials tended a sacred fire that was always kept burning. A central ritual was the Green Corn ceremony held every summer, an important feature of which was a kind of handball match with up to a thousand players. Members of the higher class were required to marry commoners. When they died, the commoner, along with several servants, was killed to accompany them in the afterlife. The highest rank of nobles was called "little suns" and was made up of the brothers and uncles of the Great Sun. The Natchez believed that those who lived well would go to a paradise after death, while those who lived badly would end up in a hell full of mosquitoes.

Natchez women's arts included baskets and mats decorated with dyed geometric patterns, incised (designs carved in their surface) pottery, cloth woven from the inner bark of the mulberry tree, and beadwork, including beaded belts used to encode important information. Men made carved and painted figures and black stone pipes.

After 1716, the Natchez, already drastically weakened by imported diseases, fought a series of wars with the French. In 1729, acting with British encouragement, Natchez raiders destroyed several French settlements, killing many people. The French, aided by the Choctaw, retaliated in force, overrunning the Natchez villages and, in 1731, capturing the last Great Sun. Those Natchez who were not killed or sold into slavery scattered among Chickasaw, Cherokee, and Creek communities. In the nineteenth century, a number of Natchez accompanied the Cherokee and Creek to Oklahoma, where they formed some small eastern communities. A few of their descendants survive near Braggs and Concharty, Muskogee County; a few other Natchez descendants are said to live among the multiethnic Summerville Indians of South Carolina. The last native speaker of the Natchez language died in 1965, and the last tribal ceremony was held in 1975. The Natchez tribe as such has effectively become extinct, with no recognized communities remaining. However, Census 2000 recorded 87 people identified as solely Natchez, with a total of 386 respondents. The 128-acre (52-ha) site of the Natchez Grand Village has been opened as a museum, with a reconstructed Natchez Indian house and three ceremonial mounds. Two of the mounds, the Great Sun's Mound and the Temple Mound, have been excavated and rebuilt to their original sizes and shapes.

Left and Above: **Today, the Grand Village of the Natchez Indians is a National Historic Landmark administered by the Mississippi Department of Archives and History. The Natchez are descendants of the Mound Builders and the Natchez Grand Village is reconstructed around three large ceremonial mounds. The site is open seven days a week and annual events include the Natchez Powwow, whose dancers can be seen here.**

Below: **A Seminole group, Florida, c. 1895. A few of the Seminole people escaped removal to Indian Territory by surviving in the dense southern Florida swamplands. Before the twentieth-century development of their distinctive patchwork quilting, they had adopted European-type clothes fashioned in unique styles, with these horizontal bands of contrasting colored cloth stitched to coats and skirts.**

The name Seminole comes from a Creek word that means "seceder" or "runaway." The tribe consisted initially of refugee Lower Creeks from the Chattahoochee and Flint Rivers, Georgia, along with Oconee, Yamasee, and Miccosukee of the Hitchiti group, who occupied the area of northern Florida following the destruction of the Apalachee people. Most spoke either Muskogee or Hitchiti, two members of the Muskogean language family. They seem to have become known as Seminole from about 1775. As the newly independent United States pressured the Creeks for additional land, more of them fled from the hostilities in the Alabama and Georgia areas into what was still Spanish territory. These later immigrants, mostly true Creeks

(Muskogee speakers) from the Upper Creek villages, tripled the Seminole population following the "Red Stick War" of 1813–14. Spanish Florida also provided a refuge for numerous escaped slaves. Although the Seminole owned a few slaves themselves, escapees were usually welcomed to their villages.

State militias often pursued runaway slaves into Florida. This issue, together with exaggerated fears of an Indian and African-American alliance across the border, provided an excuse for a more substantial invasion in 1817–18, when African-American and Seminole towns in present Jefferson County were looted and destroyed. The Seminoles retreated south, but by 1819, Florida had passed to the United States by treaty, and in 1823, the Seminoles agreed to move farther south to a tract of land that was to be a reservation in central Florida. In 1832, the Treaty of Payne's Landing, which was signed by some unrepresentative and unauthorized chiefs, committed the Seminoles to relocation to Indian Territory, now Oklahoma. As many as two-thirds of the 1,500 Seminole who were rounded up and forced to march west died from starvation, disease, or attacks along the route. The survivors formed one of the "Five Civilized Tribes," settling by the 1860s in present Seminole County, Oklahoma. Their subsequent history is much the same as that of the neighboring Creeks.

In Florida the remaining Seminoles persisted with stubborn irregular warfare, although they were continually driven south into the deep swamps (the Second Seminole War, 1836–42). Their leader, Osceola, seized while under a flag of truce, was taken to Fort Moultrie in Charleston, South Carolina, where he died in 1838. The war ended with a few hundred Seminole Indians and a handful of African-Americans still

Below: **A warrior chief of the Second Seminole War, 1835–42, by which date Seminole clothing was a unique blend of Native and European materials. The belt, garters, and perhaps the sash echo ancient prototypes seen on figures engraved on shell objects from Spiro Mound, Oklahoma, though by this date they were made of trade wool and beads. The buckskin moccasins are a form of the classic eastern one-piece center seam type. The bandolier and pouch (usually with a triangular flap) are probably derived from both Native and European models. The Native breechcloth and leggings were made in both buckskin and cloth at this date. The cut of the cloth smock-coat is thought to be of European inspiration, though buckskin prototypes may have existed in the southeast. Crescent-shaped gorgets (neck ornaments) of silver or other metals were traded or made from coins. Part of the uniform insignia of the eighteenth- and early nineteenth-century European military officer, the gorget was widely popular among the eastern peoples.**

free in the southern swamps, primarily because the government tired of a campaign that had cost over $30 million and the deaths of more than 1,500 soldiers. Sporadic attempts to remove the remaining Seminoles by force or persuasion continued throughout the nineteenth century, including what is known as the Third Seminole War in 1855–58. Another 100 or so were relocated to Indian Territory, but about 300 others took advantage of the inhospitable swampland to remain undefeated south of Lake Okeechobee. There they survived on hunting, fishing, and trading craft items until the Florida state government began to drain the swamps around the early 1920s. By this time, many of the Florida Seminoles had been converted to Christianity by Indian Baptist missionaries from Oklahoma. Most settled on reservations (the Brighton, Immokalee, and Big Cypress federal and state reservations, plus land along the Tamiami Trail) before 1940 and took up cattle or citrus fruit farming or jobs in the local towns.

The Florida Seminoles still perform the sacred Green Corn Dance and have also developed colorful quilted clothing that has become popular with tourists. A small number of Everglades Mikasuki speakers, who regarded the Seminole on the reservations as having abandoned their traditions, campaigned for separate status and in 1962 secured federal recognition as the Miccosukee Tribe. Numbering about 400, they now have their own

Below: **The Seminole chief Billy Bowlegs, from a daguerreotype, c. 1858. A leader during the Third Seminole War (1855–58), he wears a silver headband with traded ostrich feathers, and bandoliers of braided wool and beadwork.**

reservation in Dade and Broward Counties, with a population in recent years of 94 people. The Seminole Tribe of Florida has around 2,000 members and today gains the bulk of its income from gaming, sales of tax-free cigarettes, and tourism. The Mikasuki and Muskogee languages are still spoken, and there now is a rebuilt traditional-style village where regular ceremonies take place.

Most Oklahoma Seminoles (who number about 11,000) still live in Seminole County. Two "square grounds" are still used for traditional Green Corn festivals and ball games, but most Seminoles are Baptist or Presbyterian and fully integrated into the economic life of the wider society of Seminole County. Unemployment is high, with few jobs available in the area. A total of $16 million was won in a land claims case in 1976, but its use was delayed by disputes lasting many years. The Muskogee language is still spoken and many aspects of cultural traditions and heritage are maintained.

Above: **A Seminole woman sewing a colorful skirt, c. 1950. The arrival of hand-cranked sewing machines in the camps of the Florida Seminoles during the 1890s transformed their clothing. They began using bands of horizontally sewn multicolored cloth or "patchwork." The craft continues today with sales to tourists along the Tamiami Trail in southern Florida.**

CENSUS 2000

The numbers recorded for the Seminole were:

Florida Seminole	493
Oklahoma Seminole	374
Seminole	11,556
Dania Seminole	3
Total	12,431

Above: **Seminole man, c. 1880. Turbans were popular with Seminoles and men of other southeastern tribes during the nineteenth century; figurines recovered through archaeology point to their use in aboriginal times. The form shown was made by folding and wrapping a commercial woolen shawl; they were sometimes decorated with silver and plumes.**

ACOLAPISSA

A Muskogean tribe reported by French colonial governor Jean-Baptiste Le Moyne de Bienville in 1699. Living along the Pearl River, Louisiana, they may have been descended from the Napochi of the sixteenth century. In 1702, they moved to Lake Pontchartrain. Another people, the Tangipahoa, on the river of that name in Louisiana, were probably an associate tribe. During the eighteenth century, they seem to have moved to the Mississippi above New Orleans and merged with the Bayogoula and Houma.

ADAI

A Caddoan tribe formerly located near present Robeline, Natchitoches Parish, Louisiana. They met French explorer Pierre Le Moyne d'Iberville in 1699. Missions were later established among them but were destroyed by the French in 1719. By 1805, they lived at Lake Macdon near the Red River; and in about 1830, the last of them joined other southern Caddoans and merged into a composite group, the "Caddo," losing their separate identity. Another small tribe, the Eyeish, lived on Ayish Creek, a tributary of the Sabine in northeastern Texas. They were visited by the Spanish in 1542, but by the early nineteenth century they were extinct or had joined other related groups. The Adai, Eyeish, Natchitoches, Hasinai, and Kadohadacho constituted the southern branch of the Caddoan family.

APALACHEE

A powerful—7,000 strong—Muskogean tribe of northern Florida, between the Aucilla and Ochlocknee Rivers around St. Marks. They were gathered by the Spanish into collective and defenseless mission towns, which were gradually destroyed by the Creeks and Yuchi (under British influence) from South Carolina, with a final invasion in 1702–04. The balance seem to have moved to Mobile Bay and then to Louisiana or Oklahoma, where a few remained in the nineteenth century; now extinct.

ATAKAPA

A group of tribes who lived on the Gulf coast of Louisiana and eastern Texas from Vermilion Bay to Galveston Bay, including the Akokisa on the Trinity River, Texas; the Atakapa proper on the Neches, Sabine, and Calcasieu Rivers; an Eastern Atakapan group on the Mermentau River; and the Vermilion Bayou Opelousa near present Opelousas, Louisiana. Later the Bidai, Deadose, and Patiri—small groups on the middle course of the Trinity River, Texas—were added. The Atakapa first encountered explorers from Spain and France. In 1779, the eastern Atakapas helped Spanish expeditions against the British. They had sold most of their lands to the French Creoles by the early nineteenth century, however, and ultimately disappeared. The Atakapa in the Calcasieu Parish area near Lake Charles, Louisiana, held together longer, and the few remaining members of the tribe were visited and had their language recorded by ethnologists Gatschet (1885) and Swanton (1907–08). A few Creoles and "Sabines" of the area claim their ancestry. Of the Texas branches nothing is known after about 1805. They are perhaps distantly related to the Tunica and Chitimacha.

BAYOGOULA

A people of Bayou Goula, Iberville Parish, Louisiana, visited by Iberville in 1699. They seem to have been connected with the Mugulasha and Quinipissa, perhaps with the Acolapissa, as divisions of a single tribe numbering perhaps 1,500 in 1650. During the eighteenth century, they seem to have merged with the Houma.

BILOXI

A small Siouan enclave among the Muskogeans, located on the lower Pascagoula River and near Biloxi, Mississippi, where they met French explorers Iberville and Bienville in 1699, but they may have come from the north not long before. The Moctobi and Capinans were possibly subgroups. A number of their descendants are merged with the Louisiana Choctaw at Jena, La Salle Parish, Lecompte, Rapides Parish, and among the mixed Tunica-Avoyel-Ofo-Choctaw remnants in Avoyelles Parish.

CALUSA

An Indian people of southern Florida, including all the groups south of Tampa Bay to the Florida Keys and in the interior around Lake Okeechobee. They were visited by the

GREEN CORN CELEBRATION

The most important religious festival known in modern times in the southeast is the Green Corn celebration, or Busk as it is called by Oklahoma Creeks. This is a corn (maize) festival, and it was related to similar ceremonies practiced by Native peoples from the Seminole of Florida all the way to the Iroquois in the North. The Green Corn celebration was an occasion of forgiveness, amnesty, and absolution from crime; it lasted four to eight days and was performed in the town square, the "square grounds" of the present Oklahoma Creeks. The ceremony itself involved the taking of emetic drinks, which produced vomiting to ceremonially cleanse the body, and the lighting of a new fire constructed of logs pointed toward the four sacred directions. This "world renewal" ceremony probably has ancient origins and may be another legacy of the Mississippian culture.

Today, green corn festivals are held in the spring in many locations around the southeast.

Spanish as early as 1513, but missionary attempts do not seem to have been successful and were finally abandoned in 1569. The Calusa were nomadic hunters and fishermen moving from place to place with nature's cycle. Despite their isolation they must have diminished rapidly in population from perhaps 3,000. A few remained until the Seminole came into Florida, and some probably joined them or finally crossed to Cuba. They are now extinct and are presumed to have been of Muskogean connection, perhaps closest to the Choctaw, or the Timucua. The following tribes were probably connected with them: Ais, Guacata, Jeaga, and Tekeska.

CAPE FEAR INDIANS
The name given to the Indians on the Cape Fear River, North Carolina, who probably knew the early voyagers and may have been friendly to early European settlements in the area. They probably numbered several hundred in 1600 and about 200 in 1715. A few of the so-called Summerville Indians of South Carolina claim their ancestry today.

CHAKCHIUMA
A Muskogean people of the Choctaw group, in contact with Spanish explorers (1540–41) and later with French settlers in Louisiana. They seem to have lived around Leflore County in Mississippi at the junction of the Yazoo and Yalobusha Rivers. During the eighteenth century, they were at war with the Choctaw and Chickasaw, with whom their survivors probably united (or they may possibly have joined the Houma).

CHATOT
First in contact with the Spanish in 1539, west of the Apalachee on the lower reaches of the Apalachicola and Chipola Rivers of northern Florida. They suffered the same fate as the Apalachee and moved to Louisiana in the eighteenth century, where a few remained later on the Sabine River, but nothing more is known of them. They numbered perhaps 1,000 in Spanish colonial days.

CHERAW or SARA
A tribe originally located close to Chattooga Ridge, in the northwestern corner of what is now South Carolina, when first contacted by Spanish explorers. In 1670, they were

living on the Yadkin River, North Carolina, and later moved near the southern boundary of Virginia. The last of them seem to have joined the Catawba, and a number may possibly have merged with the Indians of the Lumber River. They are thought to have been of Siouan connection and numbered 510 in 1715. The Yadkin tribe, reported on the river of the same name in 1674, may have been the same or a closely related people.

CUSABO

A Muskogean people of the coast of South Carolina between Charleston and Savannah, Georgia, and along the Ashley, Edisto, and Coosawhatchie Rivers. The Guale on the Georgia coast, the lower Savannah River, and St. Catherine's Island, in contact with the Huguenot colony at Port Royal from 1562, seem also to be connected with them. The Spanish from St. Augustine, Florida, made several attempts to missionize the Cusabo until the arrival of English settlers in 1670. They seem ultimately to have joined the Catawba, Creek, or Florida Indians, although a large multiethnic group known as the Summerville Indians, who live in and around Dorchester County, South Carolina, may be partially descended from them, particularly from the Edisto River group. Spanish missionary influence on the Guale towns alternated with periods of warfare, thereby reducing them to submission until their virtual extinction in the eighteenth century.

ENO-SHAKORI

Probably two separate tribes: the Eno on the Eno River in Orange and Durham Counties, North Carolina, and the Shakori in Vance, Warren, and Franklin Counties, who may have been identical to the Sissipahaw. They apparently merged in one village called Adhusheer in about 1700. Although they were encouraged to join other groups closer to the Virginia settlements for protection, the last report of them was in South Carolina, when they probably united with the Catawba.

HASINAI

A Caddoan confederacy of small tribes of northeastern Texas, including the Anadarko and Hainai, living on the upper Neches, Trinity, and Angelino Rivers in

THE "TRAIL OF TEARS"

The "Great Removal" of the tribes of the southeast to Indian Territory (see pages 10–11) was accompanied by great suffering. The Choctaw walked to Oklahoma during the winter of 1831–32—the coldest since 1776. Over 1,600, a tenth of the population, died as a result of the enforced emigration— and the outbreak of cholera that accompanied it. In 1832, a treaty was signed with the Creek Nation that led to their removal, and by 1860, they had lost about forty percent of their population. In 1838, it was the Cherokee's turn to leave their homes—or, rather, the concentration camps into which they had been herded prior to deportation. The Cherokee call this journey the "Trail of Tears," and during it at least a quarter of the Cherokee population of 16,000 died. The Seminole also negotiated a treaty of removal. Signed in 1832, it was repudiated by a great portion of the tribe under Chief Osceola who forced the United States to fight a costly war (over $20 million) until he was arrested under a flag of truce in 1837.

Below: **A Caddo grass lodge.**

Nacogdoches, Rusk, and Cherokee Counties. They encountered the Spanish in the sixteenth century, the survivors of the La Salle expedition in 1687, and were under the control of the Spanish missions after 1690. They later moved west to the San Antonio area, to a reservation on the Brazos River in 1855. By 1859, their remaining members were united with the Kadohadacho as a composite group called "Caddo" in southern Oklahoma, where their descendants remain.

HITCHITI
A substantial group of Muskogean-speaking tribes occupying the area around the Chattahoochee and Flint Rivers in Georgia, also at various times the Apalachicola River in northern Florida. During the eighteenth century, they became associated with the Lower Creeks and ultimately shared their fate. The original tribes were the Hitchiti proper, Apalachicola, Sawokli, Okmulgee, Oconee, Tamali (Tamathli), Chiaha, Mikasuki, and probably the Osochi. After forming the "Lower Creeks" during the eighteenth century, some Oconee and Tamathli, and later Mikasuki, moved to Florida and became one of the two Seminole groups still associated with southern Florida.

HOUMA
A Muskogean tribe possibly descended from the Chakchiuma; when they first met the French in the seventeenth century they lived on the east side of the Mississippi River in Wilkinson County, Mississippi. Later they established themselves near New Orleans, where they remained throughout most of the eighteenth century around Ascension Parish, Louisiana. During the nineteenth century, they moved into the more inaccessible areas of Terrebonne and Lafourche Parishes, where their descendants, virtually all French-speaking Creoles, are still reported—Census 2000 numbered the United Houma Nation at 6,798. In earlier times, they may also have absorbed the Acolapissa tribes and the Okelousa, a tribe reported in the eighteenth century, possibly descended from an ancient people of De Soto's time.

KADOHADACHO or CADDO
The largest of the southern Caddoan confederacies who lived in northeastern Texas and adjacent Arkansas and

Oklahoma, particularly around the Great Bend of the Red River near present Texarkana. They probably knew the Spanish and French before the establishment of La Harpe's trading post in about 1719, which cemented permanent contact with whites. They provided a bulwark against the northern Indians and suffered as a consequence, withdrawing to the vicinity north of Shreveport, Louisiana. In 1835, the Caddo ceded their lands to the United States and moved to Texas, scattering and joining the Hasinai, Cherokee, and Chickasaw. Those with the Hasinai on the Brazos River were removed in 1859 to Indian Territory, where their descendants still live in the vicinity of Binger, Caddo County, now Oklahoma. They perhaps numbered 2,400 in 1700. In 1872, the composite "Caddo," including Natchitoches and Hasinai, numbered 392; in 1944, 1,165 Caddo were reported, and 1,207 in 1970, although now mostly of mixed descent through marriage with Euro-Americans and Wichitas. Census 2000 reported 2,675 Caddo, including 72 for the Caddo Indian Tribe of Oklahoma and 301 Caddo Adais Indians.

KEYAUWEE

A tribe found in 1701 near present High Point, Guildford County, North Carolina. Despite reported plans to join the Saponi and Tutelo closer to the settlements around Albemarle Sound, the last reports of them were in 1761, when their town was located close to the boundary of the two Carolinas. They are classified as Eastern Siouans.

MANAHOAC

A small tribe, possibly of Siouan extraction, who lived along the upper Rappahannock River in northern Virginia, numbering perhaps 1,000. They apparently joined the combined Saponi, Occaneechi, and Tutelo, but nothing else seems to be known of them after 1728.

MOBILE

The largest of a group of Muskogean tribes who occupied an area around Mobile Bay, Alabama, when first in contact with the Spanish, from whom they suffered heavy losses in a 1540 battle. Later they were farther north in Wilcox

Above: **Caddoan grass house. Early French and Spanish reports indicate long use of this type by the ancestors of the Wichita and Caddo of Arkansas, Oklahoma, Texas, and Louisiana, in semipermanent villages of up to eighty houses. They made a circle of heavy cedar beams supported by a secondary circle of lighter poles leaning in against them, then drawn and tied together at the apex. Horizontal ribs secured the construction, with long grass thatch tied to the ribs in overlapping layers. Communal lodges may have been as tall as 25 feet (8 m), family lodges smaller. They have not been in use since c. 1900, but there are a few reconstructions at "Indian City," Anadarko, Oklahoma.**

County, returning closer to Mobile during the French occupation. They numbered several thousand in the sixteenth century but perhaps only 1,000 by the mid-eighteenth century, combined with others. Their ultimate fate is unknown, but they perhaps merged with the Choctaw. The Tohome on the west bank of the Tombigbee River, Washington County, Alabama, and the Naniaba were probably subdivisions or closely related. They gave their name to "Mobilian," a trade jargon used in the Gulf region.

MONACAN
A group of small tribes who held the upper valley of the James River in Virginia. First contacted by English colonists in 1607, they were still living separately as late as 1702. A few people of Amherst County, Virginia, still claim their ancestry. They may have been of Siouan descent.

MONETON
An ancient tribe west of the Blue Ridge in Virginia and the Kanawha River, West Virginia. They seem to have met Europeans first in 1671, but subsequently they disappeared or merged with other tribes. On circumstantial evidence they have been grouped with the Eastern Siouan tribes.

NAHYSSAN
A small tribe contacted in 1670 while living on the Staunton River, Virginia. Their history was probably essentially similar to that of the Saponi and Tutelo.

NATCHITOCHES
A small confederacy of Caddoan tribes in northwestern Louisiana, principally along the Red River from the present city of Natchitoches to Shreveport. The Yatasi were the largest subtribe of the group. In 1700, Bienville reported 400 to 450 members. Later they descended the Red River closer to French settlements and probably united with French Creoles, or joined their relatives the Hasinai in Texas. They are no longer a separate group.

OCCANEECHI
A small tribe who lived near Clarksville in Mecklenburg County, southern Virginia. They seem ultimately to have joined the Saponi and Tutelo in the eighteenth century,

and nothing further is known of them. They are thought to have been of Siouan stock by their association with the Tutelo.

OFO

A small tribe of probably Siouan extraction who are believed to have descended the Mississippi River by 1673 from southwestern Ohio, where they were known at one time to the French as Mosopelea. By 1686, some of them were with the Taensa, and as late as 1784, had a separate village above Point Coupée, Louisiana. A small group are supposedly merged into a mixed group of Indian descendants near Marksville, Louisiana.

PASCAGOULA

A tribe closely associated with the Biloxi but perhaps of Muskogean connection, on the Pascagoula River in Jackson, George, and Perry Counties, Mississippi. Visited by Bienville in 1699, they later moved to Louisiana with the Biloxi and merged with local Choctaw in the nineteenth century.

PEDEE

A small tribe of supposed Siouan connections who lived on the Great Pee Dee River, South Carolina, and were most probably closely related to the Cape Fear and Waccamaw. A few mixed-descent people survived until the end of the eighteenth century. The name Pedee is presently used by Lumbees living in Marlboro and other counties of South Carolina, but they have no connection with the old Pedee.

PENSACOLA

A small Muskogean tribe, apparently of the Choctaw dialectic division, who occupied Pensacola Bay in northwest Florida and who first met the Spanish in the sixteenth century. By the time the Spanish post at Pensacola was established in 1698, however, they had moved inland and presumably westward. Their remaining members merged with other groups, perhaps the Choctaw.

SAPONI

A tribe originally from near Lynchburg, Virginia, thought to be of the Siouan family. Two groups of mixed-descent

Above: **Timucua man, c. 1562. From paintings by Jacques Le Moyne, cartographer and artist to the French Huguenot colony on the St. John River, of the Timucua peoples in the fortified towns of northern Florida, 1562–64. Their men had distinctive hair styles, wore feather crowns and ear plugs, were heavily tattooed, and seem to have used metal ornaments.**

people survive not far from their old territory, in North Carolina in Person, Warren and Halifax Counties; called Haliwa, these claim Saponi ancestry. During the twentieth century, a splinter of the Haliwa lived near Lancaster, Pennsylvania. Census 2000 reports 3,452 Haliwa-Saponi.

SISSIPAHAW

A group who lived on the Haw River, North Carolina. Lawson and Barnwell noted them, and later connected them with the Shakori. They apparently united with other tribes during the Yamasee War of 1715 against the English, after which nothing is known of them.

TAENSA

A Muskogean tribe, related to the Natchez, who lived near present St. Joseph in Tensas Parish, Louisiana, and who encountered the explorer La Salle in 1682. They moved several times during the eighteenth century, ultimately merging with the Chitimacha. Another group known as Little Taensa, or Avoyel, in the neighborhood of Marksville, Avoyelles Parish, Louisiana, and apparently closely related, were mentioned by Iberville in 1699. A small mixed-descent Indian group combined with Tunica, Ofo, Biloxi, and Choctaw still survived in the area in recent years.

TIMUCUA or UTINA

A collective term for the Indians of northern Florida, probably of the Muskogean family, possibly a separate family. They lived in large houses grouped in permanent towns with extensive cornfields surrounding their villages. They probably numbered 13,000 when De Soto passed through their land in 1539, followed by French settlers who were supplanted in turn by Spanish in 1565. They were gradually conquered by the latter and missionized by Franciscans. They rebelled in 1656 and suffered from pestilences which raged in the missions at various times. The remaining Timucua were concentrated into missions near St. Augustine, Florida, but continued to be harassed by northern Indians and the English. The last of them were in Volusia County, Florida, in 1736, probably becoming incorporated into the Seminole. The following tribes were perhaps associated with them: Acuera, Fresh Water Indians, Icafiu, Mocoçco,

Ocale, Pohoy, Potano, Saturiwa, Surruque, Tacatacuru, Tocobaga, and Yustaga.

TUNICA

The Tunican linguistic family consisted of a small group of tribes that occupied the valley of the Mississippi close to where the present states of Louisiana, Arkansas, and Mississippi adjoin. They comprised the Koroa on the lower Yazoo but were often reported in other locations: the Yazoo, also on that river; the Tiou on the upper Yazoo, but ultimately united with the Natchez after having been driven from their homes; the Grigra on St. Catherine's Creek, Mississippi, also adopted by the Natchez; and the Tunica proper, a few miles north of the junction of the Yazoo River with the Mississippi. They were probably visited by early Spanish and French explorers, and missionary priests were in contact with them from 1699. They were usually firm friends of the French and suffered at the hands of the Natchez as a consequence. After 1731, they gradually decreased in numbers, some remaining in their old haunts, others combining with other tribes, until some time between 1784 and 1803, when their combined survivors moved to an area near Marksville in Louisiana, near the Red River. Here, a small tribally- and racially-mixed group has survived until recent times. The whole group probably numbered about 2,500 before suffering the effects of European diseases, and by the early eighteenth century perhaps only a few hundred were left. The census of 1910 gave 48 "Tunica"; and in recent years, about 200 Indian people of mixed descent are reported from Avoyelles Parish, Louisiana, including a few occupants of the old Marksville Reservation. They are, however, of Ofo, Avoyel, Biloxi,and Choctaw, as well as Tunican ancestry. The extension of the language family to include tribes other than the Tunica proper is largely circumstantial, although some authorities have suggested a connection with the Chitimacha and, perhaps, with the Atakapan tribes on the Gulf coast of Louisiana.

TUSKEGEE

A Muskogean people, probably related to the Alabama group. They were known at various times in several locations, mostly in Alabama, including the Tennessee

Below: **Tunica chief Bride les Oeufs is depicted as part of a European conception of a Native scene in this drawing by Alexandre DeBatz of 1732.**

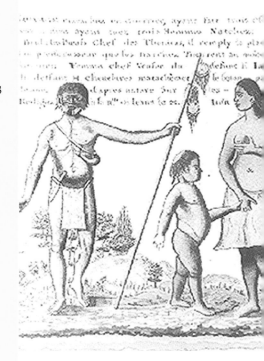

River in the northern part of the state, on the Chattahoochee near Columbus, and near Fort Toulouse (Alabama Fort) on the junction of the Coosa and Tallapoosa Rivers, when they established themselves as an Upper Creek faction.

TUTELO

A name given to several tribes around Salem, Virginia. Their survivors, along with others, were settled at Fort Christanna on the Meherrin River in 1714 and ultimately journeyed north to be formally adopted by the Cayuga in New York in 1753. Later their descendants moved to the Six Nations Reserve in Ontario, where the last full-blooded Tutelo died in 1871, and the last speaker, John Key, in 1898—though not before their language had been recorded.

WACCAMAW

A small group of Indians, probably of the Siouan family, who lived on the Pee Dee River, South Carolina, about one hundred miles northeast of Charleston. The Woccon may have been a division of the same people. It is possible that a number of their descendants are included in the Lumbee of Robeson County, North Carolina; and about 300 people of mixed descent perpetuate the name Waccamaw near Lake Waccamaw in Columbus and Bladen Counties. The Winyaw were very probably connected with them in ancient times.

WATEREE

Probably the most powerful tribe of central South Carolina at the time of the Spanish settlement at St. Helena, they lived on the Wateree River below present Camden. Their involvement in the Yamasee War of 1715 caused their ultimate decline; but they remained as a separate tribe until 1744, when they sold their remaining lands to a white trader and disappeared from history.

YAMASEE

The most important Muskogean tribe of eastern Georgia, probably connected dialectically with the coastal tribes, although the Yamasee were always located inland on the Ocmulgee River above its junction with the Oconee. They are probably the "Altamaha" mentioned in 1540 and were in contact with Spanish missions in Florida in the seventeenth century, when some moved down to St. Augustine. They later appear in South Carolina in 1715 when a tragic war broke out between them and the English colonists, which sadly largely destroyed them. A few of the Yamasee ultimately joined the Seminoles and Creeks; a mixed-ancestry group has survived in Burke County, Georgia, until recent times, although their connection with the old Yamasee is still unverified. This group is sometimes reported as "Altamaha-Cherokee" and numbers around 100.

YUCHI

An important southeastern tribe of Georgia who apparently lived in a number of locations including present-day Tennessee but are usually associated with Georgia and South Carolina, particularly the Savannah River country and even northern Florida. At various times they lived with the Creeks on the Ocmulgee, Chattahoochee, and Tallapoosa Rivers during the eighteenth century. Their language is classified as either a separate linguistic family or a very divergent Muskogean branch. In general culture they were similar to the Creek. The Yuchi moved to Indian Territory in two main groups: one identified with the Lower Creeks (McIntosh party), which arrived at Fort Gibson in 1829, and a larger party with the Upper Creeks from Alabama in 1836. During the Civil War, they divided in sentiment between Union and Confederacy, basically echoing the old Lower and Upper Creek alliances. There were four Yuchi settlements in Indian Territory, near Depew, Kelleyville, Bristow, and Mounds. In recent times, they have been concentrated around Sapulpa and Mounds and were reported to number 1,216 in 1949, although often counted among the general Creek population. The Yuchi still have two square grounds where they hold annual Green Corn dances in summer, one near Bixby, the other near Kelleyville. The Westo and Stono may have been Yuchis in conflict with the Carolina settlers in 1664 and 1669–71.

CENSUS 2000	
The numbers recorded for the Yuchi were:	
Yuchi	291
Tia	7
Anstohini/Unami	4
Total	302

Below: **The Tunica-Biloxi Museum in Markesville, Louisiana, contains a large collection of Native American and European artifacts from the Colonial period of the Mississippi valley.**

GLOSSARY

Allotment. Legal process, c. 1880s–1930s, by which land on reservations not allocated to Indian families was made available to whites.

Acculturation. Cultural modification of an individual, group, or people by adapting or borrowing the cultural traits or social patterns of another group.

Anthropomorphic. Having the shape of, or having the characteristics of, humans; usually refers to an animal or god.

Appliqué. Decorative technique involving sewing down quills (usually porcupine) and seed beads onto hide or cloth using two threads, resulting in a flat mosaic surface.

Apron. Male apparel, front and back, which replaced the breechcloth for festive clothing during the nineteenth and twentieth centuries.

Bandolier bag. A prestige bag with a shoulder strap, usually with heavy beadwork, worn by men and sometimes women at tribal dances. Common among the Ojibwa and other Woodland groups.

Birch bark. Strong, thick bark used for canoes and various wigwam coverings. Used as well for a wide variety of containers that were also adapted for the European souvenir trade by the addition of colored porcupine quills, such as those produced by the Mi'kmaq and by the Ojibwa and Odawa of the Great Lakes area. Bark was an important resource, especially in the East, North and Northwest.

Buckskin. Hide leather from animals of the deer family—deer (white-tailed deer in the East, mule deer in the West), moose, or elk (wapiti)—used for clothing. Less commonly used for dress were the hides of buffalo, bighorn sheep, Dall sheep, mountain goat, and caribou.

Bureau of Indian Affairs (BIA). Begun in 1824, transferred from the War Department to the Department of the Interior in 1849. Now, around half of the BIA's employees are Native American, and the Bureau provides services through its agencies in many big cities as well as on rural reservations.

Cacique. The chief or leader of a Native American tribe in the Southwest and other areas dominated by Spanish culture.

Confederacy. A group of peoples or villages bound together politically or for defense (e.g., Iroquois, Creek).

Cradles. Any of three main devices used across the continent to transport or carry babies: the cradle board of the Woodland tribes (cloth or skin attached to a wooden board with a protecting angled bow), the baby-carrier of the Plains (a bag on a frame or triangular hood with a cloth base folded around the baby), and the flat elliptical board covered with skin or cloth, with a shallow bag or hide straps, of the Plateau.

Drum or Dream Dance. A variation of the Plains Grass Dance adopted by the Santee Sioux, Chippewa, and Menominee during the nineteenth century. Among these groups the movement had religious features that advocated friendship, even with whites.

Ethnographer. An anthropologist who studies and describes individual cultures.

Hairpipes. Tubular bone beads made by whites and traded to the Indians, often made up into vertical and horizontal rows called breastplates.

Kachinas. Supernatural beings impersonated by costumed Pueblo peoples in religious ceremonials. Dressed kachina dolls instruct children to recognize the different spirits.

Leggings. Male or female, covering ankle and leg to the knee or thigh (male), usually buckskin or cloth.

Medicine bundle. A group of objects, sometimes animal, bird, or mineral, etc., contained in a wrapping of buckskin or cloth, that gave access to considerable spiritual power when opened with the appropriate ritual. Mostly found among the eastern and Plains groups.

Moiety. A ceremonial division of a village, tribe, or nation.

Pan-Indian. Describes the modern mixed intertribal dances, costumes, powwows, and socializing leading to the reinforcement of ethnic and nationalist ties.

Parfleche. A rawhide envelope or box made to contain clothes or meat, often decorated with painted geometrical designs.

Peyote. A stimulant and hallucinogenic substance obtained from the peyote buttons of the mescal cactus.

Peyote Religion. The Native American Church, a part-Native and part-Christian religion originating in Mexico but developed among the Southern Plains tribes in Oklahoma, which has spread to many Native communities.

Powwow. Modern celebration, often intertribal and secular, held on most reservations throughout the year.

Prehistoric. In a Eurocentric view of American Indian archaeology, Indian life and its remains dated before A.D. 1492.

Rawhide. Usually hard, dehaired hide or skin used for parfleche cases, moccasin soles, shields, and drum-heads.

Reservation. Government-created lands to which Indian peoples were assigned, removed, or restricted during the nineteenth and twentieth centuries. In Canada they are called reserves.

Roach. A headdress of deer and porcupine hair, very popular for male war-dance attire, which originated among the eastern tribes and later spread among the Plains Indians along with the popular Omaha or Grass Dance, the forerunner of the modern War and Straight dances.

Secularization of Missions. The 1834 breakup of California's Spanish missions, whereby Indians who had been forced to accept Catholicism and to labor at the missions were freed from service. Land that had been taken from the Indians was not returned as promised, however, but was instead distributed to Spanish settlers and other landowners.

Sinew. The tendon fiber from animals, used by Indians and Inuit as thread for sewing purposes.

Sweat lodge. A low, temporary, oval-shaped structure covered with skins or blankets, in which one sits in steam produced by splashing water on heated stones as a method of ritual purification.

Termination. Withdrawal of U.S. government recognition of the protected status of, and services due to, an Indian reservation.

Tobacco or pipe bag. Bags, usually buckskin, beaded, or quilled with fringing, made by most Plains peoples for men to carry ceremonial tobacco and pipes.

Tribe. A group of bands linked together genetically, politically, geographically, by religion, or by a common origin myth; a common language is the main reason. "Tribe" is itself a word that arouses controversy, with many preferring "Nation" or "People." Some "tribal" groups are only so described as a convenient tool for ethnographers studying collectively fragmented groups or collections of small groups of peoples who themselves recognized no such association.

Wampum. Clam shells or beads carved from the shells that were strung into belts and used by Native peoples as currency or strung in a pattern to record messages, documents or history.

War dance. Popular name for the secular male dances that developed in Oklahoma and other places after the spread of the Grass Dances from the eastern Plains-Prairie tribes, among whom it was connected with war societies. Many tribes had complex war and victory celebrations.

Weir. A brush or wood fence, or a net, set in a river to catch fish.

Wickiup. A rounded hut used in the West and Southwest, made from a rough frame covered in brushwood, grass or reed mats.

MUSEUMS

The United States naturally has the largest number of museums, with vast holdings of Indian material and art objects. The Peabody Museum of Archaeology and Ethnology at Harvard University, in Cambridge, Massachusetts, has over 500,000 ethnographic objects pertaining to North America, including a large number of Northwest Coast pieces. Many collections of Indian artifacts in major U.S. institutions were assembled by ethnologists and archaeologists who were working for, or contracted to, various major museums, such as Frank Speck and Frances Densmore for the Smithsonian Institution, Washington, D.C., or George Dorsey for the Field Museum of Natural History, Chicago.

Since the sixteenth century, the material culture of the Native peoples of North America has been collected and dispersed around the world. These objects, where they survived, often found their way into European museums, some founded in the eighteenth century. Unfortunately, these objects usually have missing or incomplete documentation, and because such material was collected during the European (British, French, Spanish, Russian) and later American exploration, exploitation, and colonization of North America, these collections may or may not accurately represent Native cultures. Collectors in the early days were usually sailors (Captain Cook), soldiers (Sir John Caldwell), Hudson's Bay Company agents, missionaries, traders, or explorers.

During the twentieth century, a number of museums have developed around the collections of private individuals. The most important was that of George Heye, whose museum was founded in 1916 (opened 1922) and located in New York City. It was called the Museum of the American Indian, Heye Foundation. This collection has now been incorporated into the National Museum of the American Indian, a huge building sited on the Mall in Washington, D.C., scheduled to open in September 2004. Other notable privately owned collections subsequently purchased or presented to scholarly institutions are the Haffenreffer Museum Collection at Brown University, Rhode Island; much of Milford G. Chandler's collection, which is now at the Detroit Institute of Arts; Adolph Spohr's collection at the Buffalo Bill Historical Center, Cody, Wyoming; and the impressive Arthur Speyer collection at the National Museums of Canada, Ottawa.

Many U.S. and Canadian museums and institutions have been active in publishing popular and scholarly ethnographic reports, including the Glenbow-Alberta Institute, the Royal Ontario Museum, Toronto, and, pre-eminently, the Smithsonian Institution, Washington, D.C. Most of the major U.S. museums have organized significant exhibitions of Indian art, and their accompanying catalogs and publications, often with Native input, contain important and valuable information.

In the recent past, a number of Indian-owned and -run museums have come into prominence, such as the Seneca-Iroquois National Museum, Salamanca, New York; the Turtle Museum at Niagara Falls; Woodland Cultural Centre, Brantford, Ontario, Canada; and the Pequot Museum, initiated with funding from the Pequots' successful gaming operation in Connecticut. The Pequots have also sponsored a number of Indian art exhibitions. Many smaller tribal museums are now found on a number of reservations across the United States.

There has also been much comment, debate, and honest disagreement between academics (Indian and non-Indian alike), museum personnel, and historians about the role of museums and the validity of ownership of Indian cultural material in what have been, in the past, non-Native institutions. Certain Indian groups have, through the legal process, won back from museums a number of funerary and religious objects, where these have been shown to be of major importance to living tribes or nations. The Native American Graves and Repatriation Act of 1990, now a federal law, has guided institutions to return artifacts to Native petitioners; some, such as the Field Museum of Chicago, while not strictly bound by this law, have voluntarily returned some remains and continue to negotiate loans and exhanges with various Native American groups. A listing of U.S. museums with Native American resources may be found at http://www.hanksville.org/NAresources/indices/NAmuseums.html.

FURTHER READING

Birchfield, D. L.(General Ed.): *The Encyclopedia of North American Indians,* Marshall Cavendish, 1997.

Brody, H.: *Maps and Dreams*, Jill Norman and Hobhouse Ltd, 1981.

Bruchac, Joseph: *Journal of Jesse Smoke: A Cherokee Boy: Trail of Tears, 1838*. Scholastic, Inc., 2001.

Buller, Laura: *Native Americans: An Inside Look at the Tribes and Traditions,* DK Publishing, Inc., 2001.

Coe, R. T.: *Sacred Circles: Two Thousand Years of North American Indian Art;* Arts Council of GB, 1976.

Cooper, Michael J.: *Indian School: Teaching the White Man's Way,* Houghton MIfflin Company, 1999.

Davis, M. B. (Ed.): *Native America in the Twentieth Century;* Garland Publishing, Inc., 1994.

Dennis, Y. W., Hischfelder, A. B., and Hirschfelder, Y: *Children of Native America Today,* Charlesbridge Publishing, Inc., 2003.

Despard, Yvone: *Folk Art Projects - North America*, Evan-Moor Educational Publishers, 1999.

Downs, D.: *Art of the Florida Seminole and Miccosukee Indians*, University Press of Florida, 1995.

Duncan, K. C.: *Northern Athapaskan Art: A Beadwork Tradition*, Un. Washington Press, 1984.

Ewers, J. C.: *Blackfeet Crafts*, "Indian Handicraft" series; Educational Division, U.S. Bureau of Indian Affairs, Haskell Institute, 1944.

Fenton, W. N.: *The False Faces of the Iroquois*, Un. Oklahoma Press, 1987.

Fleming, P. R., and Luskey, J.: *The North American Indians in Early Photographs*, Dorset Press, 1988.

Frazier, P.: *The Mohicans of Stockbridge*, Un. Nebraska Press, Lincoln, 1992.

Gidmark, D.: *Birchbark Canoe, Living Among the Algonquin*, Firefly Books, 1997.

Hail, B. A., and Duncan, K. C.: *Out of the North: The Subarctic Collection of the Haffenreffer Museum of Anthropology*, Brown University, 1989.

Harrison, J. D.: *Métis: People Between Two Worlds*, The Glentsaw-Alberta Institute in association with Douglas and McIntyre, 1985.

Hodge, F. (Ed.): *Handbook of American Indians North of Mexico*, two vols., BAEB 30; Smithsonian Institution, 1907–10.

Howard, J. H.: *Reprints in Anthropology Vol. 20:The Dakota or Sioux Indians*, J and L Reprint Co., 1980.

————: *Shawnee: The Ceremonialism of a Native American Tribe and its Cultural Background*, Ohio University Press, 1981.

Huck, B.: *Explaining the Fur Trade Routes of North America*, Heartland Press, 2000.

Johnson, M. J.: *Tribes of the Iroquois Confederacy*, "Men at Arms" series No. 395; Osprey Publishing, Ltd, 2003.

King, J. C. H.: *Thunderbird and Lightning: Indian Life in Northeastern North America 1600–1900*, British Museum Publications Ltd., 1982.

Lake-Thom, Bobby: *Spirits of the Earth: A Guide to Native American Symbols, Stories and Ceremonies*, Plume, 1997.

Lyford, C. A.: *The Crafts of the Ojibwa*, "Indian Handicrafts" series, U.S. BIA 1943.

Page, Jack: *In the Hands of the Great Spirit: The 20,000 Year History of American Indians,*The Free Press, 2003.

Paredes, J. A. (Ed.): *Indians of the Southwestern U.S. in the late 20th Century*, Un. Alabama Press, 1992.

Press, Petra, and Sita, Lisa: *Indians of the Northwest: Traditions, History, Legends and Life*, Gareth Stevens, 2000.

Rinaldi, Anne, *My Heart Is on the Ground: The Diary ol Nannie Little Rose, a Sioux Girl, Carlisle Indian School, Pennsylvania, 1880* (Dear American Series), Scholastic Inc., 1999.

Scriver, B.: *The Blackfeet: Artists of the Northern Plains*, The Lowell Press Inc., 1990.

Sita, Lisa: *Indians of the Northeast: Traditions, History, Legends and Life*, Gareth Stevens, 2000.

————: *Indians of the Great Plains: Traditions, History, Legends and Life*, Gareth Stevens, 2000.

————: *Indians of the Southwest: Traditions, History, Legends and Life*, Gareth Stevens, 2000.

Swanton, John R.: *Indian Tribes of the Lower Mississippi Valley and Adjacent Coast of the Gulf of Mexico*; BAEB 43; Smithsonian Institution, 1911.

Early History of the Creek Indians and Their Neighbors; BAEB 73; Smithsonian Institution, 1922.

————: *Indians of the Southeastern United States*; BAEB 137; Smithsonian Institution, 1946.

————: *The Indian Tribes of North America*; BAEB 145; Smithsonian Institution, 1952.

Waldman, Carl: *Atlas of The North American Indian*, Checkmark Books, 2000.

Wright, Muriel H.: *A Guide to the Indian Tribes of Oklahoma,* Un. Oklahoma Press, 1951.

This index cites references to all six volumes of the Native Tribes of North America set, using the following abbreviations for each of the books: GB = Great Basin and Plateau, NE = Northeast, NW = North and Northwest Coast, PP = Plains and Prairie, SE = Southeast, SW = California and the Southwest.

ABOUT THE CONTRIBUTORS

Dr. Duncan Clarke (Contributing Author)

Clarke has a master's degree from London University's School of Oriental and African Studies and has recently completed his PhD., focusing on the history of textiles in the Yoruba region of Nigeria. He is currently working as a freelance writer and lecturer on ethnic art and as a dealer in antique textiles.

Michael G. Johnson (Author)

Johnson has researched the material culture, demography, and linguistic relationships of Native American peoples for more than thirty years, through academic institutions in North America and Europe and during numerous field studies conducted with the cooperation and hospitality of many Native American communities. He has published a number of books, in particular the Denali Press Award-winning *Encyclopedia of Native American Tribes*.

Richard Hook (Illustrator and Contributing Author)

An internationally respected professional illustrator specializing in historical and anthropological subjects for more than thirty years, Hook has had a lifelong interest in Native American culture that has inspired his remarkable artwork. He has been widely published in the United States, Europe, and Japan. A lifelong interest in Native American culture led to his selection as illustrator for the Denali Press Award-winning *The Enyclopedia of Native American Tribes*.